God's Goodness
through
the
Biblical Holidays

Melanie Moscovich

ISBN: 978-1-907929-63-2

Contact Melanie at: mm.moscovich@gmail.com
http://:mmmoscovich.wix.com/book

Ip

www.lifepublications.org.uk

Dedication

To my husband Ofer and children,
Koren, Adi and Gideon

God's Goodness through the Biblical Holidays

Commendations

Melanie Moscovich has done a service in writing this informative book. For those interested in the Biblical background to their faith in Yeshua and also in the festivals that are still central to Jewish life this will make a helpful introduction. There is much here that is thought provoking and will likely whet the appetite of those who will then desire to delve deeper.

Dr Yohanan Stanfield.
Founder of 'Lech L'cha' Israeli Discipleship Ministry

Melanie Moscovich has a heart to share her belief in Yeshua as God's anointed Messiah and Saviour of all who put their trust in him. *God's Goodness through the Biblical Holidays* successfully bridges the gap between the Biblical Holidays and the ministry and teaching of Yeshua.

The book begins with a brief explanation of the Festivals in the Hebrew Calendar and then subsequent chapters explore the tradition and spiritual meaning of each Holiday. It describes how Jewish people have celebrated the Holidays. This is then related to the teaching and ministry of Yeshua, setting out the evidence for the belief that Yeshua is the Messiah before exploring how the Holiday can relate to Christians today.

This is more than a carefully factual exploration of the Holidays; we are invited to engage in a relationship with the covenant God of Abraham, Isaac and Israel, the creator of all things through prayer.

Reverend Denise Binks,
Presbyter, Methodist Church

Melanie and I have been friends since we met at college one day in a corridor over 30 years ago. Since that time, I have watched in awe as God has taken her (and her whole family) on an adventure with Him which only a loving Heavenly Father could have planned! I count it a privilege to write this commendation and it is such a delight for me to commend both Melanie and her book to you.

Melanie writes this book on Biblical Holidays from a unique perspective, having lived in Israel. Throughout she gives the historical background to each holiday and the way in which Jews around the world, both past and present, celebrate them. She then digs deeper in order to help the reader understand what they reveal about God's nature and His extravagant love for both Jew and Gentile. I have enjoyed reading about each Biblical Holiday and trust that you too will glean much from its pages. Thank you, Melanie, for taking the time to "unwrap" the significance of these holidays!

Rebecca Boucker. Elder,
Golden Valley Church, Gloucester

Melanie Moscovich has written a captivating and easy-to-read book about the celebrations and historical contexts of Biblical holidays. Melanie's passion and love for God has really shone through in her explanations of each of the holidays, of which have personally helped me in my continuing journey with God. I would highly recommend this book to anyone who is looking to learn more about the significance of the Biblical holidays and the amazing power and character of God at work in each of them. God has been given so much glory in this book, something which is equally heart-warming and inspiring to read!

Ambra Vivian, University of Gloucestershire
Christian Union President (2020/21)

Contents

Introduction

There is so much to learn from the Biblical holidays. The Lord calls them *"My appointed festivals" (Leviticus 23:2)* and he reveals something of himself to all believers through his festivals.

God set times throughout the year as appointed times, *Moadim,* to meet with his people. The festivals are special occasions for God to spend time with his people and remind them of his love and goodness to them and his involvement in their lives. God's people acknowledged his goodness and faithfulness in these times with joy and celebration. The word for holiday is *Hag* in Hebrew which means a time for rejoicing. Within the holidays there were also times for fasting and praying in repentance. Throughout the different festivals God brought his people Israel close to him to strengthen their relationship with him.

God wants to teach everyone something about himself and his love for all people through the holidays. His plan to reach all people and to be in relationship with them is demonstrated throughout the holidays. Spiritual truths and lessons given through the festivals are relevant to all of us and a blessing for all Christians to understand. We gain insight into why and what Jesus taught during the holidays and the spiritual fulfilment he achieved through these festivals. Our understanding of the

Bible is deepened and our appreciation of God's incredible love for us is too.

At the Council of Nicea in 325AD, the Early Church Fathers decided to move Good Friday and the Easter holiday away from Passover in order to separate Christians from the Biblical Holidays and Hebrew calendar. This was done to prevent Christians from celebrating the holidays, even though the early disciples did celebrate them. Something spiritually was sadly lost to the Church through this. Yet the Lord is recalling his Word and has been restoring Biblical heritage back to all his people.

The Biblical Holidays and the Hebrew Calendar

The Hebrew Calendar consists of the Biblical Holidays and other Jewish Holidays. It also relates to the agricultural seasons in Israel. There are twelve months in the calendar. A new month begins at the start of each new moon. The calendar follows both the cycle of the moon and the cycle of the sun to ensure the festivals fall into the correct season of the year for the agricultural harvests. The Hebrew calendar has 354 days in a year and an extra month which is called *Adar Bet* is added about every three years to balance the moon and sun cycles.

In the Bible the first month is called *Aviv*, which is the month when the Hebrew people left Egypt during the Exodus. *Aviv* means 'spring' and it was during the spring time that the people of Israel left Egypt. Passover holiday is celebrated in this month. It is called *Aviv* in the Scriptures although this month is also called *Nisan* in the Hebrew calendar.

The Hebrew calendar actually begins with the seventh month in the Bible, which is called *Tishrei*. It starts with the seventh month because it is believed that this was the month that God created the world and therefore is the starting point for counting the years. Each New Year takes place in the month of *Tishrei*.

A new day begins at sunset when there are three stars visible in the sky and goes through until sunset the following day in the evening. This follows the description given in Genesis,

> *"there was evening and there was morning, the first day" (Genesis 1:5).*

13

The first day of the week is called *Yom Rishon* in Hebrew. It begins on Saturday evening after sunset. The Shabbat is the seventh day of the week and is the day of rest. The Lord rested after creation on the seventh day. It starts at sunset on Friday and ends after sunset the next day. Shabbat is described as a holy day and time for a sacred assembly in Leviticus 23 which is similar to the Biblical festivals.

The number seven, which is a holy number, features in several places in the Biblical holidays. The Passover and the Feast of Tabernacles festivals are both seven-day holidays in Israel. Pentecost which is the Feast of Weeks takes place seven weeks after Passover and the days in between these two holidays are counted. The High Holidays, which are the Feast of Trumpets, Day of Atonement and the Feast of Tabernacles, all take place in the seventh month.

Added to this seven occurs in calendar cycles as well, the seventh day is the day of rest. The seventh year is a Sabbatical year when the land was left fallow and a Jubilee year occurred after seven times seven years, in other words on the fiftieth year.

The first Holiday in the Bible is the Holiday of Passover. I have started this book with two chapters on Passover to fully appreciate what Jesus achieved at this festival and the layout is slightly different from the other chapters. I have also added the Holiday of *Hanukkah* at the end of the book, although it is not one of the Biblical holidays with instructions described in the Bible it is celebrated and valued in the Hebrew calendar by Jewish people. It is worth reading about especially as it is mentioned in the New Testament in the book of John as the Feast of Dedication.

I have included writing about the way Jewish people celebrate the Holidays to give some cultural and historic background. I also hope it will help build understanding in relationships between Christians and Jewish people. Messianic Jews celebrate the Biblical Holidays with many of the traditional customs as well as celebrating in a way that reflects their faith in Yeshua, and that honours Jesus and what he taught in the Holidays.

The Biblical Holidays Calendar

Hebrew Month	Holiday	Gregorian Month
Nisan (Aviv)	14th: Pesach – Passover	March/April
Iyar		April/May
Sivan	6th: Shavuot – Pentecost	May/June
Tamuz		June/July
Av		August
Elul		August/September
Tishrei	1st: Rosh Hashanah – New Year 10th: Yom Kippur – Day of Atonement 15th: Sukkot – Feast of Tabernacles	September/October
Heshvan		October/November
Kislev	(2nd: Hanukkah – Feast of Dedication)	November/December
Tevet		December/January
Shvat		January/February
Adar	14th: Purim – Feast of Lots	February/March

Chapter 1

Passover – *Pesach*

To Him who divided the Red sea, His love endures forever.
Psalm 136

Introduction

Passover is the first of the Lord's festivals described in the Bible. It is also the first holiday God gave to the people of Israel and represents the beginning of Israel becoming God's people and a nation.

It is a holiday that is so valuable to us, as believers in Jesus the Messiah, because of what Jesus achieved at the holiday.

The Passover that took place in Egypt in which God delivered the people of Israel from slavery, *(Exodus 12)* pointed to a more powerful, prophetic event that would take place in the future, in which God would bring about the greater deliverance of all people. It is enriching to understand and review the Exodus story to know how this holiday relates to our spiritual freedom. God not only set the people of Israel free, he set all his people free through Passover. Jesus' death at Passover changed history for ever.

The holiday is referred to in many places in the Bible, in both the Old and New Testament, Exodus, Leviticus, Deuteronomy, Ezekiel, Matthew, Mark, Luke, John, Acts, 1 Corinthians and 1 Peter.

The Passover holiday has several names; Passover *Pesach*, the Holiday of Unleavened Bread *Hag ha Matzot*; Spring holiday *Hag Aviv* and the Holiday of Freedom *Hag ha Hearut,* all of which are aspects of the holiday.

The people of Israel were required to go up to Jerusalem each year to celebrate the Passover there and Jesus celebrated the Passover in Jerusalem *(Luke 2:41-42).*

The holiday is celebrated in the month of *Aviv* in the Bible. *Aviv* means spring time and the actual Passover happened in spring. It takes place on the 14th day of the month and it lasts for one week beginning with a celebratory meal called the *'Seder'* meal on the first evening of the holiday. The *Seder* meal was the Lord's last supper *(Mark 14:12-16).*

The Biblical and historical background of the holiday

The Exodus of the Hebrew people from Egypt took place over 3000 years ago. The Hebrew people had been slaves for 430 years, *(Exodus 12:40-41).* God had seen the suffering and the misery of the Hebrew slaves and he sought to intervene. He chose Moses to lead them out of slavery into freedom instructing him to tell Pharaoh to let the Hebrew people go free.

The name Passover comes from the passages in the Bible where the angel "passed-over" the homes of the people of Israel sparing them from the plague of the killing of the first born.

As Moses went to deliver this message to Pharaoh, a powerful spiritual battle began, with God revealing and displaying his power and authority as the only one true God.

We know from the Passover narrative that Pharaoh had been told by an Egyptian astrologer much earlier that one day a Hebrew male would rise up and lead the Hebrew people to freedom. Pharaoh, being afraid of this, ordered the killing of all Hebrew boys by having them thrown into the Nile.

Yocheved, one of the Hebrew mothers, hid her baby son in a papyrus basket sealed with tar and placed it in the Nile. She told her daughter Miriam to watch over the basket in the hope that someone would take pity on the baby boy and take care of him. Pharaoh's daughter found the basket with the baby inside and took him out of the water. She named him Moses which means 'I drew him out of the water'.

Miriam saw Pharaoh's daughter rescuing Moses and went quickly to her offering to get a Hebrew wet nurse to nurse the baby. She fetched her mother Yocheved who was then able to take care of her son for three more years.

Moses grew up in Pharaoh's palace, raised by Pharaoh's daughter. As a young man he defended a Hebrew slave from a beating by a slave master. He struck the slave master killing him. Following that Moses fled from Egypt to Midian where he met Zipporah, a Midianite shepherdess and they got married. He worked as a shepherd for forty years and whilst tending sheep in the desert Moses had an encounter with God.

A bush was burning but was not consumed by the fire. Fearfully he walked towards the burning bush and he heard God's voice speaking to him.

> *When the Lord saw that he had gone over to look, God called to him from within the bush, "Moses! Moses!" And Moses said, "Here I am." (Exodus 3:3)*

> *The Lord said, "I have indeed seen the misery of my people in Egypt. I have heard them crying out because of their slave drivers, and I am concerned about their suffering." (Exodus 3:7)*

> *God said to Moses, "I am who I am. This is what you are to say to the Israelites: 'I am has sent me to you.'" (Exodus 3:14)*

> *I have promised to bring you up out of your misery in Egypt into the land...flowing with milk and honey. (Exodus 3:17)*

God told Moses to go to Pharaoh and tell him to let his people go,

> *Then say to Pharaoh, "This is what the Lord says: 'Israel is my firstborn son, and I told you to let my son go, so that he may worship me.'"*
> *(Exodus 4:22-23)*

Moses did not want this task of telling Pharaoh to let the Israelites go, he said his speech was slow. God told him he gives man speech and that Aaron his brother would help him.

Moses returned to Egypt with his family and together with Aaron they went to Pharaoh and told him to let the Hebrew slaves go. Pharaoh resolutely refused and in retaliation made the Hebrew slaves work even harder than before. As slaves they were building the cities of Pithom and Rameses. Pharaoh then forced them to collect the straw as well, to make the bricks and the slaves resented Moses for making their labour harder.

Moses returned to Pharaoh to tell him to let the Hebrew people go and again Pharaoh refused. God then started to demonstrate his power and authority over Pharaoh. He told Moses to throw down his staff and it immediately turned into a snake. Pharaoh's magicians tried to show similar power and they did the same but Aaron's staff swallowed up their staffs (*Exodus 7:8-12*).

God repeatedly showed he was more powerful than any Egyptian spiritual power. He did this through the signs of the ten plagues. He turned the river Nile to blood, sent frogs, lice, flies, and caused disease amongst the livestock. He sent boils, hail, locusts and darkness over the land and then the final, fatal plague on the firstborn of the land.

The Egyptian magicians at first tried to match God's power. They also turned the Nile into blood and they also sent frogs just as God had done but they were unable to turn the blood back to water and they were unable to get rid of the frogs.

Pharaoh told Moses if he got rid of the frogs, he would then let the Hebrew people go to worship their God in the desert. However once Moses got rid of the frogs, Pharaoh changed his mind and refused to let the people go.

God hardened Pharaoh's heart throughout the course of the plagues, for the purpose of a greater display of signs and wonders demonstrating God's power.

Amid these plagues, God showed his love and protection over his people by protecting the land of Goshen where the Hebrew people lived.

During the course of nine plagues Moses told Pharaoh to let the Hebrew people go. Then, before the last and most fatal plague, Moses told the Hebrew people to prepare to leave. He instructed them to slaughter a lamb and put the blood of the lamb on their door posts and lintel in order to protect them from the final plague.

> *The blood will be a sign for you on the houses where you are, and when I see the blood, I will pass over you. No destructive plague will touch you when I strike Egypt. (Exodus 12:13)*

The Hebrew people were instructed to eat the roasted lamb and to prepare bread without yeast as there was no time for the bread to rise because they had to leave in haste that night.

God struck Egypt with the final plague by slaying the first born child and animal of every family. Pharaoh was awakened that night with the terrible wailing in Egypt. Not one home was left without someone dead. He summoned Moses and Aaron and told them to leave with all the Hebrew slaves, but to bless him first. That night, the Bible tells us six hundred thousand men left Egypt in haste *(Exodus 12:37)*. The total number is estimated to be two million people to include the number of women and children who also left during the night that spring. God led his people by a pillar of cloud by day and a pillar of fire by night.

In the hardness of his heart, Pharaoh changed his mind yet again and ordered the Egyptian soldiers to pursue the Hebrew people that same night. The Hebrew slaves as they fled were then confronted with the frightening situation of facing the water of the sea in front of them and the Egyptian army closing in behind them with nowhere else to turn.

The pillar of cloud which had been in front of the people of Israel moved to the back of the people separating them from the Egyptian army bringing light to the Hebrews and darkness to the Egyptian army. God told Moses to stretch out his hand over the sea and through the night the Lord drove the sea back by a strong wind, so all the Hebrew people were able to cross on dry land, with a wall of water on each side. Then God told Moses to stretch out his hand again over the water as the Egyptian army pursued them. The water of the sea returned and all the Egyptian army drowned *(Exodus 14:15-31)*. The people of Israel were finally free to follow God.

Lessons God taught through the holiday of Passover

He is a God of relationships, love and compassion

God showed his character and his nature. First of all and foremost he showed he wanted to be in relationship with his people and to be their God.

> *"I will take you as my own people, and I will be your God." (Exodus 6:7)*

He also expressed his love and compassion for them,

> *"The Lord said, 'I have indeed seen the misery of my people…and I am concerned about their suffering.'"* *(Exodus 3:7)*

God demonstrated he cared about the struggles people go through and that he intervened into their situation, changing their history.

> *"Then you will know I am the Lord your God, who brought you out from under the yoke of the Egyptians." (Exodus 6:7)*

God is the only God and he reigns over the supernatural

God brought the ten plagues to show Pharaoh and the Egyptian people, as well as the people of Israel, that he is the only real God. It is estimated that the plagues took place over the course of a year in which God displayed his supernatural power.

God publicly undermined the power the Egyptian people believed their gods had. When God brought darkness over the land he undermined the Egyptian sun god *Ra*. He did the same to *Apis*, the bull god, when he sent the plague on the livestock. The Egyptians depended on the river Nile for water for their crops and economy. They turned to *Heqt* the river god of the Nile to provide for them and by turning the Nile into blood God showed that *Heqt* had no power.

The first two plagues the Egyptian magicians tried to match with counterfeit plagues but they could not reverse what God had done, nor could they match any other plagues.

With the last plague, the God proved his power over death. As the Hebrew people put the blood of the slaughtered lamb on their door posts and lintels for protection, God proved that the Egyptian gods could not protect the people against death, only he could.

God not only undermined the power of Egyptian gods but also the most powerful ruler at that time, Pharaoh, showing nobody could stand against his power. The Scriptures say that God raised up Pharaoh to display his power to the world.

> *"But I have raised you up for this very purpose that I might show you my power and my name might be proclaimed in all the earth."*
> *(Exodus 9:16 and Romans 9:17)*

God also revealed his supernatural power over nature through the signs and wonders of the ten plagues and by parting the waters of the sea.

> *The Israelites went through the sea on dry ground, with a wall of water on their right and on their left. (Exodus 14:22)*

His power was displayed for all to see.

God will fight for his people

God showed through the Exodus that he will fight for his people to defend them and protect them.

> *Stand firm and you will see the deliverance the Lord will bring you today. The Lord will fight for you; you only need to be still. (Exodus 14:13-14)*

He even caused their enemies to admit he is fighting for his people.

> *The Egyptians said, "Let's get away from the Israelites! The Lord is fighting for them against Egypt." (Exodus 14:25)*

People can depend on God to fulfil his plans and purposes

Moses did not want the role of speaking to Pharaoh. He felt inadequate for the task to which God was calling him. He doubted his own ability because his speech was slow. God responded by saying he gives man speech teaching Moses to depend on him and not on his own strength.

God said, "I will be with you." (Exodus 3:12)

God taught people not to depend on their natural talents and abilities to serve him, rather to respond to his calling and his promise to be with them and provide all they need to fulfil the plans he had for them.

As Moses obeyed God's calling, he had to face more opposition. The people of Israel at first resented his interference because it made their lives harder. Satan brought opposition and hardship as he came against God's plans for Moses and the Hebrew people. Moses persevered and his remarkable faith is described in the book of Hebrews *(Hebrews 11:13-29)*. The results were a people set free to become a nation of God's people to be used for his purposes.

God changes people from their old practices to a new way of life with him

During the time in the wilderness, after the Hebrew people left Egypt, they turned to idols creating the golden calf. They came out of a culture of worshipping man made idols and when Moses was away on Mount Sinai they worshipped a golden calf, which had similarities to the Egyptian bull god, *Apis*. God had to strip away this culture and to teach his way of following him as the one and only true God. The people also lacked faith in God and complained in the wilderness resulting in that generation being prevented from entering the Promised Land.

God instructed his people to remember his acts and what he had done for them

> *"Observe the month of Aviv and celebrate the Passover of the Lord your God, because in the month of Aviv he brought you out of Egypt by night." (Deuteronomy 16:1)*

Remembering God's acts and intervention brings encouragement and builds faith in God. The people of Israel have celebrated the Passover holiday ever since the Passover in Egypt, in order to remember God's intervention into their lives. God showed the importance of remembering what he has done in the past, to keep trusting him especially when new difficult times come.

God taught his people the importance of telling their children and future generations of what He has done

The story of the Exodus and Passover was to be retold every year to children so that the Passover would never be forgotten, and children would learn about God's power and deliverance. Each generation was to tell the next generation about him, so faith in God would be passed on in this way.

> *Celebrate the Festival of Unleavened bread, because it was on this very day that I brought your divisions out of Egypt. Celebrate this day as a lasting ordinance for the generations to come… And when your children ask you, "What does this ceremony mean to you?" Then tell them, "It is the Passover sacrifice to the Lord." (Exodus 12:17,27)*

27

On that day tell your son, "I do this because of what the Lord did for me when I came out of Egypt." (Exodus 13:8)

Main Message

The Passover narrative begins with slavery and ends with freedom. God demonstrated his love for the Hebrew people by setting them free to become his people and a nation. He showed his desire to be in a relationship with them. It is the first holiday the Jewish people celebrated and is a key event in their history. It was such an important holiday that all the Kings of Israel in the Bible counted the years of their reign from the time of Passover each year.

God's deliverance of the Hebrew slaves goes so much further than just their freedom. He revealed himself to Israel and the whole world as the only true God.

God had set a people free to follow him and also to bless the nations. Through Israel God would reveal his salvation to all people. He gave his written Word, the Bible, through the people of Israel and most importantly the Messiah came from them.

In his message to Pharaoh God said, *"Israel is my first born, let him go free so he may worship me."* As people from other nations entered into a relationship with God through the Messiah they became part of God's family and his children too. Like any good loving father God loves all of his children with the same love for each child. God showed his love to his first born Israel and then to many people from every nation. God's great plan to redeem all people had begun, the Exodus and Passover were part of this incredible plan.

Chapter 2

The Passover Meal

The *Seder*

*"I have eagerly desired to eat this Passover with you
before I suffer."*
Luke 22:15

For Christ, our Passover lamb was sacrificed.
1 Corinthians 5:7

The way the *Seder* is celebrated, including Jesus' teaching at the meal

The story of the Passover and the wonders of the Exodus are all retold at the Passover meal. The meal takes place in the evening. Throughout the evening the food eaten and the traditions are all to remind Jewish people of the Passover when God brought them out of slavery in Egypt into freedom to follow him and to the Promised Land. The meal follows a specific order called the *Seder*.

Jesus celebrated the Passover meal every year in Jerusalem. We see several elements of the *Seder* in his Passover meal with his disciples described in the New Testament. By looking at the Passover meal and the *Seder* we gain a deeper understanding of his teaching and a greater appreciation of what Jesus accomplished and fulfilled through his death at Passover.

> *Jesus said, "...eagerly I desire to eat the Passover before I suffer". (Luke 22:15)*

The Bible says he knew he was to give his life at Passover,

> *He said to his disciples, "As you know the Passover is two days away and the son of man will be handed over to be crucified." (Matthew 26:1-2)*

At Passover Jesus demonstrated his incredible love for people,

> *It was just before the Passover Feast. Jesus knew that the time had come for him to leave the world, he now showed them the full extent of his love. (John 13:1)*

The setting of the *Seder*

At the Passover meal families and friends come together to celebrate. People celebrated in Jerusalem following Biblical instruction, however, since the exile after the destruction of the second Temple Jewish people mainly celebrate in their homes wherever they live. The table is set with plates and cutlery that are kept just for Passover. The wine glasses are set ready for the four cups of wine or grape juice which will be drunk during the course of the evening. There is a *Seder* plate on the table which has specific food items on it each to remind people of the Passover story.

Some of the instructions are given in Exodus for the Passover meal.

> *That same night they are to eat the meat roasted over the fire, along with bitter herbs, and bread made without yeast. (Exodus 12:8)*

On the plate are:

Bitter herbs (*Maror*): usually horse radish which has a bitter taste to bring to remembrance the bitterness of being slaves in Egypt.

A shank bone of a lamb (*Zeroa*): to remember the lamb killed on the eve of the Passover in Egypt and the sacrificial Passover lamb sacrificed in the Temple at the holiday.

Parsley or lettuce (*Karpas*): a green vegetable to represent the spring time of when the Passover took place.

A sweet mixture *(Haroset):* a mixture of apples and nuts mixed with date syrup and cinnamon. The consistency reminds people of the consistency of the mortar the people had to use to make the bricks with to build the cities for Pharaoh.

A roasted egg (*Beitzah*): symbolising new life; new life for the Hebrew people set free from slavery. The egg is hard inside and also symbolises the hardness of Pharaoh's heart.

On the *Seder* table, there are bowls of salty water to dip the parsley and unleavened bread (*Matzah)* into. The salty water represents the tears shed by the Hebrew people in slavery and the crossing of the sea.

There is also a plate with *Matzah*. It is unleavened because the people of Israel had to leave in haste and did not have time for the dough of the bread to rise.

Each person sits at the table in a reclining position as a sign of freedom, in ancient times culturally only a free person could eat in a reclining position; slaves had to eat standing. The people of Israel were set free from slavery and so they could eat as free men. Jesus and his disciples followed this tradition,

> *Jesus was reclining at the table with the twelve.* *(Matthew 26:20)*

The father of the home, or the leader of the group, leads the evening service. Jesus would have led the service with his disciples.

1. *Kadesh* – the first cup of wine is filled and blessed before it is drunk

There are four cups of wine drunk over the course of the evening (a person need only drink half a cup each time)

The four cups of wine each represent the four promises God made to the people of Israel in *Exodus 6:6-7*.

The promises are as follows and each cup has a name as well,

> **I will bring you out from the burdens of the Egyptians.** The first cup, the cup of Sanctification.

I will deliver you from bondage. The second cup, the cup of Praise.

I will redeem you with an outstretched arm. The third cup, the cup of Redemption.

I will take you to be a people for me. The fourth cup, the cup of Acceptance

Everyone drinks the first cup of wine, the cup of Sanctification.

2. *Urchatz* – next the participants wash their hands.

3. *Karpas* – everyone eats some parsley or lettuce dipped into salty water.

4. *Yahatz* – there are three pieces of unleavened bread, *matzah,* on a plate. They are to remember the three forefathers Abraham, Isaac and Jacob. Remembering when Moses approached the burning bush and God said,

> *"I am the God of your father, the God of Abraham, the God of Isaac and the God of Jacob."*
> *(Exodus 3:6)*

At Messianic Passover celebrations the three pieces of unleavened bread also are used to represent the Father, the Son and the Holy Spirit.

The leader breaks the middle *matzah* into half and wraps half of it in a serviette and hides it, which is called the *Afikoman*. *Afikoman* in Greek means dessert and is kept for later. The children look for it after the meal and they are given a reward for finding it.

5. *Maggid* – telling of the story (the story of the Passover is called the *Hagada)*. The youngest child asks four questions to start the story telling,

- "Why is this night different from all other nights? On all other nights, we eat leavened bread or unleavened bread. On this night why do we eat unleavened bread only?"
- "On all other nights we eat all kinds of vegetables, on this night why do we eat bitter herbs?"
- "On all other nights, we do not dip our food and on this night why do we dip twice?"
- "On all other nights, we eat sitting or reclining, and on this night, why do we only recline?"

The retelling the story of the Exodus begins with the leader answering these questions. He starts by speaking about the unleavened bread, the *matzah.*

"This is the bread of our affliction that our ancestors ate in Egypt. This year we are slaves. Next year we shall be free. Let all who are hungry come and eat. Let all who are in need come and share the Passover meal.

"We were slaves to Pharaoh in Egypt, and the Lord brought us out from there with an outstretched arm. If the Holy One had not brought our fathers out of Egypt we and our children and our children's children would still be slaves in Egypt..."

The leader then explains the food on the *Seder* plate and what it symbolises and talks about the experiences of the Hebrew slaves in Egypt and of God's deliverance, referring to verses in the Bible. The story telling includes mentioning all the plagues by name and each person dips a finger into the wine and spills a drop on their plate at the mention of each plague;

blood, frogs, lice, gnats, flies, boils, hail, locusts, darkness, slaying of the first born. The first part of the *Hallel*, which means "praise", is read and this is Psalms 113 and 114.

At the conclusion of the story telling the second cup is drunk, the cup of Praise.

6. *Rahtzah* – the leader washes his hands a second time.

Jesus went further than the ceremonial hand washing showing the depths of his servanthood and his desire to teach his disciple that they were clean. In following his example they should serve others.

> *He got up from the meal, took off his outer clothing, and wrapped a towel round his waist. After that, he poured water into a basin and began to wash his disciples' feet... "Now that I, your Lord and teacher, have washed your feet, you also should wash one another's feet...I tell you no servant is greater than the master... Now that you know these things, you will be blessed if you do them."*
> *(John 13:4,5,14,16,17)*

7. *Motze matzah* – the leader blesses the unleavened bread and gives everyone a piece of the unleavened bread.

8. *Marror* – everyone takes the piece of the unleavened bread and dips it into the bitter herbs and eats it. It is probably at this point that Jesus told his disciples that one of them would betray him,

> *Jesus was troubled in spirit and testified, "I tell you the truth, one of you is going to betray me." One of them, the disciple whom Jesus loved, was reclining next to him.*

Simon Peter motioned to this disciple and said, "Ask him which one he means."

Jesus answered, "It is the one to whom I will give this piece of bread when I have dipped it in the dish." Then dipping the piece of bread, he gave it to Judas Iscariot, son of Simon. As soon as Judas took the bread, Satan entered into him. "What you are about to do, do quickly," Jesus told him. As soon as Judas had taken the bread, he went out. And it was night. (John 13 21,23,26-27,30)

In *Psalms 41:9* it was prophesied about the Messiah,

He who shares my bread has lifted his heel against me.

and Jesus said,

"I am not referring to all of you; I know those I have chosen. But this is to fulfil this passage of Scripture: 'He who shared my bread has turned against me.'" (John 13:8)

9. *Korech* – the participants take a broken piece of unleavened bread and put some of the bitter herbs and the sweet mixture together on it. This is to symbolise going from the bitter taste of slavery to the sweet taste of freedom.

10. *Shulhan orech* – the meal is served and eaten.

11. *Tzafun* – the half piece of unleavened bread (the *afikoman*), which was hidden by the leader earlier, is now searched for by the children and the one who finds it gets a reward. The leader breaks the *afikoman* and shares it amongst the people at the table.

Jesus took the unleavened bread, broke it and gave it to his disciples, he knew he was about to give his life to pay for sin.

And he took bread, gave thanks and broke it, and gave it to them, saying, "This is my body given for you: do this in remembrance of me." (Luke 22:19)

12. *Barekh* – the third cup of wine, which is the cup of Redemption, is blessed. It was this cup, the cup of Redemption, that Jesus used to demonstrate through his blood he would provide redemption for all mankind.

After supper, he took the cup, saying, "This cup is the new covenant in my blood: do this, whenever you drink it, in remembrance of me."
(1 Corinthians 11:25)

In Him we have redemption through his blood, the forgiveness of sins. (Ephesians 1:7)

The Lord told his disciples,

"Drink from it, all of you. This is my blood of the covenant, which is poured out for many for the forgiveness of sins." (Matthew 26:27,28)

Everyone drinks the third cup of wine.

13. *Hallel* – the next part of the Psalms would be read or sung in praise of God. These are Psalms 115-118 and include some prophetic verses about the Messiah in Psalm 118. The words were about to be fulfilled through Jesus.

I will give you thanks, for you answered me; you have become my salvation. The stone the builders rejected has become the capstone; the Lord has done this, and it is marvellous in our eyes. (Psalms 118:22)

The fourth cup of wine, the cup of Acceptance, is blessed and drunk. It is unlikely that Jesus would have drunk this cup as he said after he shared the third cup of wine with his disciples,

"I tell you I will not drink of the fruit of the vine from now on until that day when I drink it new with you in my Father's kingdom." (Matthew 26:29)

When Jesus and his disciples had finished the Passover *Seder*, it says they sang a hymn which was most likely the *hallel*, Psalms.

When they had sung a hymn, they went out to the Mount of Olives. (Matthew 26:30)

Traditionally there is a fifth cup of wine which is poured and put aside for Elijah who will herald in the Messiah. Believers in the Messiah know this was fulfilled in John the Baptist.

14. *Nirtzah* – a conclusion prayer that the Passover has been acceptable to God.

Jesus fully participated in the Passover meal. He had celebrated it every year and then at his final Passover celebration, the Last Supper, he taught so much about the sacrifice he was about to make for all people and he was preparing his disciples for what was going to happen.

How the holiday relates to Jesus' teaching and ministry and spiritual lessons we learn from the Passover Holiday

It was part of God's plan that Jesus would die at Passover. It was prophesied in the Scriptures and Jesus knew he was to give his life at this holiday. Jesus said,

This is what is written; the Christ will suffer and rise from the dead on the third day. (Luke 24:46)

What God revealed to his people at the Exodus and Passover in Egypt was a foreshadow of what Jesus would achieve at the holiday.

These are a shadow of the things to come; the reality, however, is found in Christ.
Colossians 2:17

The incredible spiritual significance of what he accomplished can be understood through Jesus' teaching and through the symbols of the Passover.

Jesus the Passover Lamb

During the Passover holiday, the priests in the Temple were required to sacrifice the Passover lambs, as a sin offering on behalf of the people of Israel and the lambs needed to be without blemish.

The animals you choose must be year-old males without defect, and you may take a sheep or the goats... Do not break any of the bones.
(Exodus 12:5,46)

Jesus was called the Lamb of God by John the Baptist.

The next day John saw Jesus coming towards him and said, 'Look, the Lamb of God, who takes away the sin of the world! (John 1:29)

Jesus was the Passover Lamb; the perfect lamb, without blemish. He was without sin and had to die to pay for the sins of all people.

The precious blood of Christ, a lamb without blemish or defect. (1 Peter 1:19)

For Christ, our Passover lamb, has been sacrificed. (1 Corinthians 5:7)

Then came the day of unleavened bread on which the Passover lamb had to be sacrificed.
(Luke 22:7)

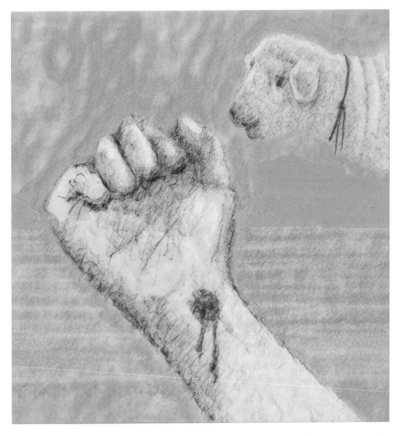

Much earlier Isaiah had prophesied about the Lamb and the coming Messiah.

He was led like a Lamb to the slaughter...though he had done no violence, nor was any deceit in his mouth. Yet it was the Lord's will for him to crush him and cause him to suffer...my righteous servant will

*justify many, and he will bear their iniquities. For he
bore the sins of many. (Isaiah 53:7, 9-12)*

In line with other scriptural teaching about the Passover lamb
not one of Jesus' bones were broken *(Exodus 12:46, Numbers
9:12, Psalms 34:20, John 19:36).*

Interestingly, when Jesus was born, angels appeared to the
shepherds in the fields tending sheep. These shepherds were
tending sheep that were being raised for Temple sacrifice,
sheep without blemishes.

The blood of the Lamb

Before the final plague the people of Israel were told to
sacrifice a lamb and to take the blood of the lamb and put it on
their door posts to protect them from the final plague: The
death of the first born.

> *Take a bunch of hyssop, dip it into the blood on the
> top and on the sides of the door-frame. When the
> Lord goes through the land...he will see the
> blood...and will pass over that doorway, and he
> will not permit the destroyer to enter your houses
> and strike you down. (Exodus 12:22-23)*

The people of Israel were required to put the blood of the
Passover lamb on their door posts to protect them from death.
Jesus' blood gives us spiritual protection from eternal death
and from the enemy's attacks.

In the book of Revelation it says they overcame Satan by the
blood of the Lamb and the word of their testimony.

> *They triumphed over him by the blood of the Lamb
> and by the word of their testimony.*
> *(Revelation 12:11)*

We sing about the power of the blood of the Lamb. We also pray the blood over our lives and over the lives of our loved ones for protection from the enemy's attacks recognising the spiritual covering his blood gives us.

Jesus' blood and the wine

Jesus lifted the third cup of wine, the cup of Redemption, and he spoke about his blood being poured out as a payment for sin.

After the supper, he took the cup, saying, "This cup is the new covenant in my blood, which is poured out for you." (Luke 22:20)

Jesus showed the symbols of the Passover meal represent the spiritual act that he was about to do to give his life to redeem people.

In him we have redemption through his blood, the forgiveness of sins, in accordance with the riches of God's grace. (Ephesians 1:7)

We have now been justified by his blood. (Romans 5:9)

The blood of Jesus Christ his son cleanses us from all sin. (1 John1:7)

Jesus' blood was the payment for sin and cleansed us from our sins. Jesus had to die for our redemption. There was no other option but the sacrifice he made,

No man can redeem life of another or give to God ransom for him, the ransom for life is costly, no

payment is ever enough…But God will redeem my life. (Psalms 49:7-8,16)

Jesus' body and the bread

During the Passover evening celebration Jesus took the unleavened bread and broke it and gave it to his disciples.

He took bread and gave thanks and broke it, and gave it to them saying, this is my body given for you. (Luke 22:19)

Jesus told his disciples that his body would be given to pay for sin. The bread that was broken at the Passover meal was unleavened bread (*Matzah*) because God had told the people of Israel to eat unleavened bread to remember leaving Egypt in haste. Jesus was breaking unleavened bread and leaven is in some places referred to as sin in the Bible *(Luke 12:1, 1 Corinthians 5:6-8)*.

Your boasting is not good. Don't you know that a little yeast works through the whole batch of dough? Get rid of the old yeast that you may be a new batch without yeast – as you really are…Therefore let us keep the festival, not with the old yeast, the yeast of malice and wickedness, but with the bread without yeast, the bread of sincerity and truth. (1 Corinthians 5;6-8)

In comparing his body to the unleavened bread Jesus was demonstrating that his body was without sin.

The Bible also tells us to examine our hearts before taking the bread and the wine.

A man ought to examine himself before he eats of the bread and drinks of the cup.
(1 Corinthians 11:28)

Taking the bread and wine at communion is a time to deeply appreciate Jesus' sacrifice for us but it is also a time of repenting of our sins. We can ask the Holy Spirit to reveal to us any sin of which we need to repent so nothing will come between our relationship with the Lord.

Reclining and Freedom

The Passover meal is eaten in a reclining, comfortable position to symbolise being able to eat as a free person. God gave the people of Israel freedom from slavery in Egypt, so they eat the meal as free people. Jesus followed this custom *(Matthew 26:20)*.

Reclining, which represents freedom, is another important message given at the Passover meal. Jesus gives us spiritual freedom from being slaves to sin by his death on the cross.

Jesus replied, "I tell you the truth, everyone who sins is a slave to sin. So, if the Son sets you free you will be free indeed." (John 8:34,36)

Freedom from sin controlling our lives is something God wants for each of us and to have true spiritual freedom we are not to allow sin to control our lives.

It is for freedom that Christ has set you us free. Stand firm, then, and do not let yourselves be burdened again by a yoke of slavery.
(Galatians 5:1)

But thanks be to God that, though you used to be slaves to sin, you have come to obey from your heart the pattern of teaching that has now claimed your allegiance. (Romans 6:17)

Passover holiday and the resurrection of Christ

Jesus said he would die and on the third day he would rise again. Death could not hold him. It was during the Passover holiday that Jesus died for our sins but also during this holiday that he rose again.

God raised him from the dead on the third day and caused him to be seen. (Acts 10:40)

Because of Jesus' resurrection we never need to fear death,

Jesus said to her, I am the resurrection and the life the one who believes in me will live, even though they die, yet they shall live. (John 11:25)

Personal

The People of Israel were told to make the Passover meal personal as if the individual had been set free *(Exodus 13:8).* Every believer is given the deep reassurance of drawing close to God in a personal, loving relationship. Through Jesus, death and sin were no longer able to separate us from a Holy God.

Since we have confidence to enter the Most Holy place by the blood of Jesus, by a new and living way opened for us...let us draw near to God with a sincere heart and with the full assurance that faith brings. (Hebrews 10:18-22)

Jesus in effect says to each one of us, "I died for the punishment of your sins and you will live in my righteousness."

*God made him who had no sin to be a sin offering for
us, so that in him we might become the righteousness
of God. (2 Corinthians 5:21)*

The Marriage Supper of the Lamb

We can see a lot of spiritual symbolism by looking at a
traditional Jewish wedding and what Jesus did at the Passover
and how it relates to the marriage supper of the Lamb
described in Revelation (*Revelation 19:6-9*). Before a
traditional Jewish wedding can take place a payment is paid by
the bridegroom for his bride. Jesus referred to himself in
several places as the bridegroom *(Mark 2:19, Luke 5:34)*. At
the Passover meal Jesus spoke about his blood being shed to
make payment for sin to redeem people, his bride.

The payment for a bride takes place at a betrothal ceremony
and a cup of wine is drunk to seal the betrothal between the
bridegroom and his bride. Jesus drank the third cup, the cup of
redemption with his disciples and he made the payment for his
bride.

In a traditional Jewish wedding setting the bridegroom then
goes away after the betrothal to prepare a home for him and
his bride with the promise he will return to get her. Jesus told
his followers he would be going back to the Father to prepare
a place for his bride.

*And if I go and prepare a place for you, I will come
back and take you to be with me that you also may be
where I am. (John 14:3)*

Jesus also told his disciples after the Passover meal that he
would not drink the fruit of the vine until he drank it with his
bride in heaven.

I will not drink from the fruit of the vine from now on until when I drink new with you in my father's kingdom. (Matthew 26:29)

In Revelation we read about the wedding supper of the Lamb when Jesus will return for his bride and be reunited with her, his people. Then the celebration of the wedding of the Lamb will take place. Amazing!

Let us rejoice and be glad and give him the glory! For the wedding of the lamb has come, and his bride has made herself ready…Then the angel said to me, write this: Blessed are those who are invited to the wedding supper of the Lamb. (Revelation 19:6-7,9)

Main Message

The depth of Jesus' spiritual accomplishment at Passover when he died and paid the price for his people, his bride, should never be underestimated or undervalued. Jesus was the Passover Lamb who was sacrificed for us. His body given and his blood poured out for each one of us to pay for our sin completes the very purpose of the holiday. He died to gain our freedom because of his love for us and the greatest freedom a person can find is to have a relationship with God. Let us remain faithful to him as we wait to celebrate the wedding supper of the Lamb truly united with him.

I remember thinking at a Passover meal in Israel how much Christians would enjoy knowing the whole spiritual picture of Passover. To know how God had a plan from the very first Passover all the way to the last Passover meal Jesus celebrated with his disciples in Jerusalem. I thought I would love to share this with brothers and sisters in the Lord.

Prayer

LORD, I thank you for the incredible price you paid in my place at the Passover. I give my life to you to be in relationship with you and follow you. I pray to live free from sin controlling my life.

Lord, I pray that the Jewish people, whenever they celebrate the Passover, would have revelation that Jesus is the true Passover lamb sacrificed for all people to have spiritual freedom. Amen.

The Passover Meal – The *Seder*

Chapter 3

Pentecost – *Shavuot*

*And they were all filled with the Holy Spirit and spoke
the word of God boldly.*
Acts 4:31

Introduction

Pentecost is the Biblical holiday called the Feast of Weeks
(Deuteronomy 16:10).

This holiday is called *Shavuot* in Hebrew, which means weeks.
God instructed the people of Israel to count seven weeks from
the Passover *(Deuteronomy 16:9).*

The forty-nine days would be counted and then the fiftieth day
was the Holiday of the Feast of Weeks. Fifty in Greek is
Pentekostos, which is where the name Pentecost comes from,
the fiftieth day after Passover.

The holiday takes place in the month of *Sivan* in the Hebrew
calendar, which is late spring time in Israel. Pentecost or
Shavuot was one of the three holidays that the people of Israel
went to worship God in Jerusalem. Jesus would have gone to
celebrate *Shavuot* in Jerusalem each year.

There are several names for this holiday in the Bible, such as Feast of the First Fruits *Yom ha Bikkurim (Numbers 28:26)* as it was the time for bringing in the first fruit of the harvest to the Lord. Another name is Feast of the Harvest *Hag Ha Katzir (Exodus 23:16),* because the holiday takes place at the spring harvest. It is also known to Jewish people as the time of the giving of our *Torah, Zman Matan Torateinu*, which is the first five books of the Bible. In the New Testament, it is called Pentecost *(Acts 2:1).* All these names reveal a significant aspect about the holiday.

In the Bible the two holidays of Passover and Pentecost are connected by the counting the weeks, but there is also an important spiritual connection between these two holidays. It is helpful for us as believers in the Messiah to understand why God connected these two holidays together.

The Biblical and historical background of the holiday

In the Bible, the people of Israel were told to count the weeks from the second night of Passover to the holiday of *Shavuot*, this is called the counting of the *Omer*. An *Omer* was a measurement of a sheaf of barley which was cut and brought into the Temple as a wave offering to the Lord.

> *From the day after Shabbat, the day you brought the sheaf of the wave offering, count seven full weeks. Count off fifty days up to the day after the seventh Shabbat and then present an offering to the Lord. (Leviticus 23:15-16)*

Count off seven weeks from the time you begin to put the sickle to the standing corn. Then celebrate the Feast of Weeks to the Lord your God by giving a freewill offering in proportion to the blessings the Lord your God has given you. And rejoice before the Lord your God. (Deuteronomy 16:9-11)

Once the counting of the *Omer* was completed, the holiday was celebrated with thanksgiving for the produce of the spring harvest.

Celebrate the Feast of Weeks with the first fruits of the wheat harvest. (Exodus 34:22)

God had taken the people of Israel out of Egypt with the Passover and brought them into the land of Israel where he blessed them by providing crops for them. They brought the first fruits of the spring harvest to him at the Temple in Jerusalem, thanking God for the harvest.

Another Biblical and historical part of the holiday was celebrating the giving of the Ten Commandments. During their journey from Egypt on their way to the Promised Land, Moses received the Ten Commandments from God at Mount Sinai.

In the third month after the Israelites left Egypt on the very day they came to the desert of Sinai...and Israel camped there in the desert in front of the mountain... Moses went down to the people and told them. (Exodus 19:1,2,25)

And God spoke all these words: "I am the Lord your God, who brought you out of Egypt, out of the land of slavery. You shall have no other gods before me." (Exodus 20:1-3)

The Ten Commandments were given in the third month, *Sivan (Exodus 20)*. The holiday of *Shavuot* was celebrated at this time and the people of Israel included celebrating the receiving the Ten Commandments as part of the holiday.

Lessons God taught through the holiday of *Shavuot*

Receiving and following the written Word of God leads to spiritual freedom

The holidays of Passover and *Shavuot* are connected by the counting of the *Omer* in the Bible and God taught an important lesson about spiritual freedom through the connection of these two holidays. First, he set his people free through the Passover, free from slavery and to be in a relationship with him. However they were not set free to go their own way, or to go back to the old ways they had followed in Egypt. The first of God's written instructions were the Ten Commandments, given at the time of *Shavuot*. The freedom they received at Passover only became true spiritual freedom when they received his instructions of how to live and be in a relationship with him. Part of his love for his people was giving them guidelines to follow showing how much God valued his people and they belonged to him.

> *The secret things belong to the Lord our God but the things revealed belong to us and to our children forever, that we may follow all the words of this law. (Deuteronomy 29:29)*

> *As for God, his way is perfect: the Lord's word is flawless; he shields all who take refuge in him. (2 Samuel 22:31)*

God's provision of the harvest

Another lesson God showed his people through the holiday of *Shavuot* was that he provides and blesses them with food at harvest time. The Feast of Weeks was a joyous occasion full of thanksgiving to God for the spring harvest. They were taught to give the first fruits of the spring harvest back to God thanking him, recognising that all gifts belong to God and come from him.

> *Bring the best of the first fruits of your soil to the house of the Lord your God. (Exodus 23:19)*

The way Jewish people celebrate *Shavuot*

At *Shavuot,* Jewish people celebrate the giving of the Ten Commandments as the start of God giving his written Word. One of the names of the holiday, *Zman Matan Torateinu* means the giving of our *Torah*. Many orthodox Jews will stay up all night reading the Word of God to appreciate the gift of his Word.

During the holiday, the book of Ruth is read in the Synagogues along with other Bible readings. The book of Ruth is read because it is set at the time of the spring harvest. Ruth arrived in Israel with her mother-in-law, Naomi, during harvest time and Ruth worked in the fields.

Ruth was a Moabite woman, a Gentile who had married a Jewish man. Her husband died in Moab and Ruth decided to go to Israel with her mother-in-law, Naomi. Naomi tried to persuade her to remain in Moab with her own family, instead Ruth accepted the God of Israel as the true God and committed her life to him,

"Where you go, and where you will stay I will stay. Your people will be my people and your God my God." (Ruth 1:16)

God honoured her commitment to follow him. Boaz, her kinsman redeemer, noticed her during the harvesting of one of his fields. When he found out about what she had done in coming to Israel he blessed her saying,

"May the Lord repay you for what you have done. May you be richly rewarded by the Lord, the God of Israel, under whose wings you have come to take refuge." (Ruth 2:12)

Boaz and Ruth married and Ruth became the great-grandmother of King David *(Ruth 4:21-22)*. By being a part of King David's family line she also became part of the line of the Messiah.

Ruth's story is one of love, friendship and faithfulness. It also shows that a Gentile woman came to believe in the God of Israel. Her story gives a glimpse into an important spiritual truth which was to come, namely that both Jews and Gentiles would worship the living God.

Psalms are read during the holiday in memory of King David and his praise of God, as it is traditionally believed that King David was born and died at *Shavuot* time.

It is customary for Jewish people to eat dairy products such as cheese cake during the holiday. The people of Israel were given dietary instructions found in *Exodus 23:19*. This led to the traditional kosher law of separating meat and dairy products. Food made from dairy products are eaten to value these kosher laws. Dishes made with wheat products are also eaten as it is a time to enjoy the produce from the spring harvest. Children have parades, holding flowers, and wearing hats decorated with flowers, giving thanks for God's provision of the produce of the land.

How the holiday relates to Jesus' teaching and ministry

In the New Testament the link between the Holidays of Passover and *Shavuot* is made again through Jesus. Jesus died at Passover, fulfilling his role as the Passover lamb, sacrificed for sin. Jesus set people free at Passover from sin and Satan through his death, but to be really free people need the Holy Spirit to enable them to lead Spirit filled lives. People need both the freedom given at Passover and the gift of the Holy Spirit given at Pentecost-*Shavuot* to truly follow God.

Before returning to heaven, Jesus told his disciples to remain in Jerusalem until the holiday of the *Shavuot* to receive the gift of the Helper, the Holy Spirit.

> *After his suffering...he gave them this command; "Do not leave Jerusalem, but wait for the gift my Father promised, which you have heard me speak about...You will receive power when the Holy Spirit comes on you." (Acts 1:3-4,8)*

> *"I am going to send you what my Father promised; but stay in the city until you have been clothed with power from on high." (Luke 24:49)*

The Holy Spirit was sent fifty days after the Passover at the Holiday of the Feast of Weeks, Pentecost.

When the day of Pentecost came, they were all together in one place. Suddenly a sound like the blowing of a violent wind came from heaven and filled the whole house where they were sitting. They saw what seemed to be tongues of fire that separated and came to rest on each of them. All of them were filled with the Holy Spirit and began to speak in other tongues as the Spirit enabled them.
(Acts 2:1-4)

The transformation the Holy Spirit brought to people

The disciples boldly shared the Gospel

The disciples were completely changed by the Holy Spirit, from being fearful after Jesus' death, to boldly sharing the Gospel leading many people to faith in Jesus. When Peter stood up and spoke about Jesus three thousand people came to believe.

Therefore, let all Israel be assured of this; God has made this Jesus whom you crucified, both Lord and Christ. When the people heard this, they were cut to the heart...Those who accepted his message were baptised, and about three thousand were added to their number that day... And the Lord added to their number daily those who were being saved.
(Acts:2:36-37,41,47)

So the word of God spread. The number of disciples in Jerusalem increased rapidly, and a large number of priests became obedient to the faith.
(Acts 6:7)

People were filled with the Holy Spirit

In several places the disciples are described as being filled with the Holy Spirit. Other people also received the Holy Spirit as the disciples placed their hands on them.

Peter, filled with the Holy Spirit said... (Acts 4:8)

Barnabas, a good man full of the Holy Spirit and faith and a great number of people were brought to the Lord. (Acts 11:24)

Peter and John placed their hands on them and they received the Holy Spirit. (Acts 8:17)

The Holy Spirit reminded people of Jesus' Words

Jesus promised that when the Holy Spirit came he would remind his followers of the words he had shared.

But the counsellor, the Holy Spirit, whom the Father will send in my name, will teach you all things and will remind you of everything I have said to you. (John 14:26)

A new revelation and understanding of the Word of God came

Many prophesies from the Old Testament came to light as the Holy Spirit revealed the meaning and significance of these prophesies to the disciples.

Peter brought a prophetic scripture, *(Psalms 16:10),* to light about the Messiah not being abandoned to the grave within the context of the holiday. He spoke about King David when addressing the crowd at Mount Zion in Jerusalem, where the tomb of David is. At *Shavuot* people were remembering King David and reading the Psalms. Peter spoke about how King David had looked forward to the coming of the Messiah referring to Jesus.

> *"Fellow Israelites, I can tell you confidently that the patriarch David died and was buried, and his tomb is here to this day. But he was a prophet and knew that God had promised him on oath that he would place one of his descendants on his throne. Seeing what was ahead, he spoke of the resurrection of seeing the Christ, that he was not abandoned to the grave, nor did his body see decay. God has raised this Jesus to life, and we are all witnesses of the fact."*
> *(Acts 2:29-32)*

Another Old Testament prophecy that was revealed and brought to life was a prophecy from Joel *(Joel 2:28-32)* when God promised to pour his Spirit on all people which is described in Acts.

> *In the last days, God says, I will pour out my Spirit on all people. Your sons and daughters will prophesy, your young men will see visions, your old men will dream dreams. Even on my servants, both men and women, I will pour out my Spirit in those days, and they will prophesy. I will show wonders in the heaven above and signs on earth below, blood and fire and billows of smoke...and everyone who calls on the name of the Lord will be saved.(Acts 2:16-19,21)*

Signs and wonders took place

> *The apostles performed many miraculous signs and wonders among the people. And all the believers used*

to meet together in Solomon's colonnade... crowds gathered also from the towns around Jerusalem, bringing their sick and those tormented by evil spirits, and all of them were healed.
(Acts 5:12,16)

Fellowships started

They devoted themselves to the apostle's teaching and to fellowship, to breaking of bread and to prayer.
(Acts 2:42)

The spreading of the Gospel began to both Jewish and non-Jewish people

Shavuot was one of the holidays when Jewish people were required to be in Jerusalem, there were Jews from many nations as well as God fearing people from other nations.

Now when the day of Pentecost came...There were staying in Jerusalem God-fearing Jews from every nation under heaven... Both Jews and converts to Judaism; Cretans and Arabs – we hear them declaring the wonders of God in our own tongues.
(Acts 2:1,5,11)

Evangelism and the spread of the gospel to the nations began. After the holiday people returned to their homes around Israel and to other nations. They took the Gospel message with them sharing it with people. God was using this holiday, when so many people from different countries were in Jerusalem, to receive and then spread the Gospel. Jesus' words about the Gospel going from Jerusalem to the ends of the earth began at Pentecost.

But you will receive power when the Holy Spirit comes on You; and you will be my witnesses in Jerusalem, and all Judea and Samaria, and to the ends of the earth. (Acts 1:8)

Repentance and forgiveness of sins will be preached in his name to all nations, beginning in Jerusalem. (Luke 24:47)

The Holy Spirit brought spiritual unity between Jews and non-Jews.

For we were all baptised by one Spirit into one body – whether Jews or Greeks, slaves or free – and we were all given the one Spirit to drink. (1 Corinthians 12:13)

The spiritual lessons of the holiday and how they apply to us today

In both the Old and New Testament, the holidays of Passover and Feast of Weeks are connected. The People of Israel were set free from the bondage of slavery but they only became free when they received God's laws and guidelines to follow. In the New Testament, Jesus died to pay for our sins at Passover setting us free from the bondage of sin, but we only become truly spiritually free when we follow God's Word and receive his Spirit given at Pentecost.

Your word is a lamp to my feet and a light for my path. (Psalms 119:105)

"I will ask the father, and he will give you another helper, who will stay with you forever." (John 14:16)

In the very same way that the Holy Spirit transformed the early disciples he transforms us too. He gives us boldness to share the gospel. He gives us revelation and understanding of the Scriptures and renews our mind by the Word of God. He will bring signs and wonders for God's glory in our day. He enables us to have true fellowship with other believers and unites people together in fellowships. He will change us to become more like Christ. We can pray for all these things knowing that God promises to give his Spirit without limit.

> *…for God gives the Spirit without limit.*
> *(Luke 11:13)*

> *…how much more will your father in heaven give the Holy Spirit to those who ask him. (Luke 11:13)*

God shows us how much he loves and values us through the Holy Spirit,

> *God has poured out his love into our hearts by the Holy Spirit whom he has given us. (Romans 5:5)*

In the light of the Holy Spirit bringing so many blessings and guidance into our lives let us be encouraged to live Spirit led lives,

> *Since we live by the spirit let us keep in step with the Spirit. (Galatians 5:25)*

The Holiday of the Feast of Weeks is also called the Holiday of First Fruits and teaches about bringing the first fruits to God in thanksgiving and worship. The people of Israel brought their first and best crops and animals to the Lord to the Temple in Jerusalem during the holiday, recognising everything belonged to God and has been given by him. We too should give our best to God, offering our first fruits in whatever way we can, in thanksgiving to God. The Bible says,

> *Honour the Lord with your wealth, with the first fruits of all your crops. (Proverbs 3:9)*

There is another aspect to the holiday of First Fruits to appreciate. Jesus died and he rose on the third day, and because of his resurrection, he is described as the first fruits,

> *But now Christ has been raised from the dead, the first fruits of those who have fallen asleep. (1 Corinthians 15:20)*

We, who believe in Jesus, are also described as First Fruits of God's creation, bringing a deeper and personal meaning to the holiday.

> *He chose to give us birth through the word of truth, that we might be a kind of first fruits of all he created. (James 1:18)*

Main Message

The Feast of Weeks, Pentecost, celebrates the giving of God's Word and the giving of the Holy Spirit. As we pray to be filled with the Holy Spirit he brings the supernatural power of God into our lives and he assures us we are loved by God. As we listen to his voice he leads us and guides us and through him we gain revelation and understanding of the Bible. We also grow in courage to share about Jesus. By the Holy Spirit's enabling we become more like Jesus and show God's love to people around us.

This holiday was very special for us as we had a dedication service for our firstborn son in a Messianic fellowship in Israel at *Shavuot*. It is a lovely holiday to dedicate children to the Lord being the holiday of bringing the first fruits to God.

Prayer

Lord, thank you for the holiday of Pentecost when we remember the giving of your Holy Spirit and your Written Word. Thank you that you promise to give your Spirit without limit. We pray to be filled by your Spirit, to become more like Jesus and to share about him. We pray that you would pour your Spirit on all people so that many would know you. Amen.

Chapter 4

The Feast of Trumpets
Rosh Hashanah

Return to me with all of your heart.
Joel 3:12

Introduction

The holiday of New Year is called *Rosh Hashanah* in Hebrew which means Head of the Year. It is known as the Feast of Trumpets in the Bible. Another name for the holiday is *Yom Truah,* which means Day of blowing the *Shofar*, it actually translates blasting the *shofar*. A *shofar* is a ram's horn. If you have ever heard the *shofar* blown, you will know it makes a very distinct "calling" sound. Instructions for the holiday are given in Numbers and Leviticus,

> *On the first day of the seventh month hold a sacred assembly and do no regular work. It is a day for you to sound the trumpets. (Numbers 29:1)*

> *A sacred assembly with trumpet blasts.*
> *(Leviticus 23:24)*

The holiday is also known as *Yom Hazikaron* meaning a Day of Remembrance, a day for Israel to remember God and turn back to him. Also it is called *Yom Hadin*, which means the Day of Judgement, as it is believed to be a time when God judges people.

The holiday takes place on the first day of the seventh month of the Hebrew calendar *Tishrei*. It may seem peculiar to start a new year in the seventh month. The sages of Israel believed that the first day of the month of *Tishrei* was the first day of Creation which they believed was in the year 3760 BC. It therefore became the starting point for calculating each New Year in the Hebrew calendar.

The holiday falls around September or October and is a special holiday because it is a celebration of people turning back to God.

Jesus would have celebrated the holiday and heard the sound of the *shofar* being blown. In the Bible the *shofar* was blown for kings and is a sound we will look forward to hearing when it will be blown to announce the return of Jesus, the King of kings.

> *For the Lord himself will come down from heaven, with a loud command, with the voice of the archangel and with the shofar – trumpet call of God.*
> *(1 Thessalonians 4:16)*

The Biblical and historical background of the holiday

The blowing of the ram's horn reminds the people of Israel of the covenant God made with them when Abraham was tested. Abraham bound Isaac for a sacrifice in obedience to God and God provided a ram instead to sacrifice.

Sometime later God tested Abraham. He said to him, "Take your son, Isaac, whom you love and go to the region of Moriah. Sacrifice him there as a burned offering"...Abraham looked up and there in a thicket he saw a ram caught by its horns. He went over and took the ram and sacrificed it as a burned offering instead of his son. (Genesis 22:1-2,13)

God tested Abraham, and Abraham showed his complete trust in God and set an incredible example by his unwavering faith in God. God made a covenant with Abraham and the people of Israel and the sound of the *shofar* – the ram's horn – became a reminder of this covenant.

The angel of the Lord called Abraham from heaven for a second time and said, "I swear by myself, declares the Lord, that because you have done this and have not withheld your son, your only son, I will surely bless you and make your descendants as numerous as the stars in the sky and as the sand on the seashore. Your descendants will take possession of the cities of their enemies, and through your offspring all the nations on earth will be blessed, because you have obeyed me. (Genesis 22:15-19)

The binding of Isaac took place on Mount Moriah, the place where the Temples were later built.

The ram's horn, *shofar,* is blown for several purposes in the Bible:

A call to repentance

It was blown at times when the nation's prophets were warning of God's coming judgement on Israel. An example of this is when the prophet Joel warned the people of Israel that judgement was coming,

71

> *Blow a trumpet in Zion; sound the alarm on my holy*
> *hill. Let all who live in the land tremble, for the day*
> *of the Lord is coming. (Joel 2;1)*

Another example is when Jeremiah warned the people of God's judgement,

> *This is what the LORD says…"I appointed*
> *watchmen over you and said, 'Listen to the sound of*
> *the trumpet!' But you said, 'We will not listen.'…I am*
> *bringing disaster on this people, the fruit of their*
> *schemes, because they have not listened to my words*
> *and have rejected my law." (Jeremiah 6:17,19)*

A call to prepare for battle and during battle

The *shofar* was blown as an audible warning of invading armies as well as during the battle to confuse the enemy. The sound of the *shofar* being blown in battle has a spiritual aspect as well to confuse Satan in battles against Israel. Joshua blew the ram's horn in the battle of Jericho.

> *"Make seven priests carry trumpets of ram's horns in*
> *front of the ark. On the seventh day, march around the*
> *city seven times, with the priests blowing the*
> *trumpets"…When the trumpets sounded, the army*
> *shouted, and at the sound of the trumpet, when the*
> *men gave a loud shout, the wall collapsed. (Joshua*
> *6:4,20)*

Gideon and his army blew ram horns in the battle against the Midianites,

> *…when Gideon and the hundred men with him*
> *reached the edge of the Midianite camp. Suddenly,*
> *they blew the ram's horn and broke their jars…and*
> *they all shouted, "A sword for the Lord and for*

Gideon!"...all the Midianites rushed around in a panic, shouting as they ran to escape. When the 300 Israelites blew their rams' horns, the Lord caused the warriors in the camp to fight against each other with their swords. (Judges 7:19-22)

At important spiritual events

The *shofar* was blown at important spiritual events, such as when God gave the Ten Commandments at Mount Sinai to Moses,

On the morning of the third day there was thunder and lightning, with a thick cloud over the mountain, and a very loud trumpet blast. Everyone in the camp trembled...only when the ram's horn sounds a long blast may they approach the mountain...And God spoke these words: "I am the Lord your God, who brought you out of Egypt, out of the land of slavery. You shall have no gods before me."
(Exodus 19:13,16, 20:1-2)

Also, when King David brought the Ark of the Covenant to Jerusalem,

So all Israel brought up the ark of the covenant of the Lord with shouts with the sounding of the ram's horns and trumpets, and of cymbals, and the playing of lyres and harps. (1 Chronicles 15:28)

In praise of God as King

The *shofar* is blown acknowledging God's kingship and in worship to him,

With trumpets and the blast of ram's horn-shout for joy before the Lord, the King. (Psalm 98:6)

At the anointing of Kings

> *Zadok the priest took the horn of oil from the sacred tent and anointed Solomon. Then they sounded the trumpet and all the people shouted, "Long live King Solomon!" (1Kings 1:39)*

At holidays and new moons

The *shofar* is blown to announce Feasts and new moons.

> *Sound the ram's horn at the New moon, and when the moon is full, on the day of our feast.*
> *(Psalms 81:3-4)*

From the time of the second Temple, (586 BC), messengers were sent around Israel and Jewish communities in surrounding countries, to let people know when the holiday was to start. They would listen for the blowing of the *shofar* at the start of the holiday and would also listen for the sound of the *shofar* during the festival.

At the holiday of the Feast of Trumpets, New Year, the *shofar* was blown as a spiritual wake up call, calling people to repentance and to return to God. God set this holiday for people to listen to the blasting of the ram's horn to remind them to turn back to him and away from sin.

There are three types of blasts on the ram's horn:

1. *Tekiah* – which means "blast" and is a long drawn out note to get worshippers, attention and is described like a siren sound. It was used at kings' coronations. There is also *Tekiah-ha gadol* the longest blast of the *shofar*.

2. *Shevarim* – which means "broken". These are three short blasts blown together. This is done at least

three times. It signifies repentance.

3. *T'ruah* – which means "alarm" or "applause" which is rapid short sharp sounds of at least nine blasts and blown to awaken the soul. In Numbers 29 it says the *shofar* is to be blown throughout the day and one hundred notes are blown. All three types of blasts are blown on the New Year.

Lessons God taught through the holiday of the Feast of Trumpets

Return and repentance

Through the holiday God taught his people the importance of repentance and returning to a right relationship with him. God instructed the people of Israel to set aside a day, free from work, when they must listen to the *shofar* as a call to spiritual reawakening and repentance. God gave this time for the people of Israel to reflect on the past year and repent of their sins and of the sins of the nation, showing the important of national repentance. This was done at the start of a New Year, so people would renew their commitment to God for the coming year.

God is Judge

God taught that he will judge people and he warns them of coming judgement if people do not repent. The sound of the *shofar* reminds the people of Israel to seek his forgiveness. It also reminds people that there will be a day of judgement when all people will be judged.

God forgives people and his desire is to be back in a close relationship with his people.

As Israel sought God in repentance and asked for forgiveness, God revealed his compassionate character to show mercy and to forgive his people. He showed his longing and hope for people to repent so that his relationship with them could be restored.

God is King

Through the holiday God taught that he is king and Creator of the world and that he rules over his creation.

The way Jewish people celebrate the holiday of the Feast of Trumpets

People listen to the sound of the *shofar* being blown on the first day of the month of *Tishrei*. The sound of the *shofar* has a compelling sound calling people to wake up spiritually and to think about their ways from the previous year and what they need to change in the coming year.

After New Year a ten day period begins for reflection and repentance which is completed on the Tenth of *Tishrei,* the Day of Atonement. The days in between these holidays are known as the Days of Awe, *Yamim Noraim* and the Days of Return, *Teshuvah.*

In Jewish traditions it is believed the Book of Life is opened at New Year and then sealed on the Day of Atonement and that God judges people at this time. Prayers of repentance are said in the hope that their names will be written in the Book of Life.

The book of Micah is read to remember God's mercy,

> *You will again have compassion on us; you will tread our sins underfoot and hurl our iniquities into the depths of the sea. (Micah 7:19)*

It is also customary for some Jewish people to go to a river bank or sea to recite *Taschlich* "casting" and throw small pieces of bread or small stones into the water as a symbolic way of remembering that God casts away their sins into the sea.

It is a time to seek forgiveness for individual sin and national sin and to pray for Israel's redemption. In the New Year service passages from Exodus are read about the sin of the golden calf. Passages from Genesis are also read reaffirming God's covenant with Israel that he made with Abraham. People also seek forgiveness from others whom they need to make amends with.

The Shabbat that falls during these ten days of repentance is called Shabbat of Return and the words from the prophet Hosea are read,

> *Return O Israel to the Lord your God. Your sins have been your downfall! Take words with you and return to the Lord. Say to him; Forgive all our sins and receive us graciously, that that we may offer the fruit of our lips. (Hosea 14:1-2)*

God's sovereignty over all mankind is also proclaimed and additional donations to charity are made recognising God's concern for all people – especially the poor and those in need.

The New Year is both a solemn and a joyful holiday. Solemn in the seriousness of the need to confess sin and joyous in a time to return to God with the assurance of a new start with God in the coming year.

In the home, Jewish families get together for a festive meal. The woman starts by lighting the candles for the holiday and reciting the blessings. People greet each other with the words "May your name be inscribed and sealed for a good New Year."

Different types of sweet food are eaten to symbolise the hope for a sweet New Year. The sweet *Challah* bread which is regularly eaten on Shabbat and other holidays is dipped into honey instead of salt.

The *Challah* is shaped into a round loaf symbolising the yearly cycle, as one year ends another begins. It also symbolises the goodness of God having no end.

Apples are sliced and dipped into honey and people bless one another saying "May it be the Lord's will to renew us for a year that is good and sweet". There is honey cake and dates which are sweet.

The word for dates is *tam-mar* and this has a double meaning at the holiday, as *tam mar* also means "bitterness has ended", expressing the hope that those who want to harm the Jewish people will be prevented from doing so and bitterness will come to an end.

Pomegranate is served at the table, as it is a fruit with many seeds and is eaten as a symbol for the many good deeds a person hopes to do in the coming year.

How the holiday relates to Jesus' teaching and ministry

Returning to God, forgiveness, spiritual reawakening, and reconciliation to God are all part of the holiday of the Feast of Trumpets, as well as acknowledging that God is Judge and King. All these lessons were part of Jesus' teaching and ministry.

Returning to God

God sent Jesus to the world to reconcile men to himself. In preparation for Jesus' coming God sent John the Baptist with a message of returning to God and the need to repent. It was prophesied in Isaiah that God would send someone to prepare people to repent and turn back to God.

> *A voice of one calling: "In the wilderness prepare the way of the Lord; make straight in the desert a highway for God." (Isaiah 40:3)*

> *In those days, John the Baptist came, preaching in the Desert of Judea and saying, "Repent, for the kingdom of heaven is near." (Matthew 3:1-2)*

Jesus said he came to reveal the Father to men, so they would know God and be in a relationship with him.

> *Jesus answered, "I am the way and the truth and the life. No one comes to the Father except through me...The words I say to you are not just my own. Rather, it is the Father, living in me, who is doing the work." (John 14:6,10)*

Through Jesus' sacrifice and death on the cross, people have the reassurance of being reconciled to God by faith in him.

....and through him to reconcile to himself all things, whether on earth or in heaven, by making peace through his blood, shed on the cross...but now he has reconciled you by Christ's physical body through death to present you holy in his sight, without blemish and free from accusation. (Colossians 1:20,22)

The message given to Israel is to return to God and of his desire to be back in relationship with his people. Jesus taught this same message and spoke of God's joy as people repent and are reconciled to him,

I tell you, there is rejoicing in the presence of the angels of God over one sinner who repents. (Luke 15:10)

Forgiveness

Seeking God's forgiveness is an important part of the Feast of Trumpets. Jesus taught about forgiveness especially through the Lord's Prayer with the need to ask for forgiveness from God and also to forgive others.

Forgive us our sins as we forgive those who sin against us. (Matthew 6:11)

Forgive and you will be forgiven. (Luke 6:73)

Spiritual reawakening

The time of the New Year is a call to spiritual reawakening and Jesus warned his disciples about the dangers of falling asleep spiritually. He gave the example of ten virgins, five of whom fell asleep. Instead he told people to be awake spiritually and alert, led by the Holy Spirit,

Be dressed ready for service and keep your lamps

burning...it will be good for those servants whose master finds them ready, even if he comes in the second or third watch of the night. (Luke 12:35,38)

In another passage the importance of spiritual awakening is shown,

Wake up O sleeper, rise from the dead, and Christ will shine on you. (Ephesians 5:14)

Jesus will return with the sound of the shofar

Jesus' return will be announced by the sound of the ram's horn, the *shofar,*

The seventh angel sounded his shofar, trumpet, and there were loud voices from heaven, which said; "the kingdom of the world has become the kingdom of our Lord and of his Messiah, and he will reign for ever and ever." (Revelation 11:15)

The spiritual lessons of the holiday and how they apply to us today

The holiday is a time for reflection and repentance when the people of Israel confessed their sin, showing how important it is to take time to reflect and return to God. We all need to recognise the importance of taking time to reflect and think about our actions and attitudes. As we open ourselves to the Holy Spirit he will reveal our sin to us and the sins of our nation that needs confessing. Repentance and returning to God is essential for staying in a close relationship with him. God's love for us is so strong he does not want any sin get in the way and hinder our relationship with him.

God promises to forgive our sins and we are reassured of his forgiveness and cleansing from the sin. This reassurance is given in both the Old and New Testament.

Though your sins are like scarlet, they shall be as white as snow: though they are as red as crimson, they shall be like wool. (Isaiah 1:18)

If we confess our sins, he is faithful and just and will forgive us our sins and purify us from all unrighteousness. (1John 1:9)

Once God has cleansed us from sin, we need to accept the reassuring truth that we can start afresh with God, with the closeness of our relationship restored and renewed.

As far as the east is from the west, so far has he removed our transgression from us. (Psalms 103:12)

This holiday reminds us that God is King and Judge and he will judge us. The people of Israel brought their individual sins and the sins of the nation to God and repented of them. We need to repent of our sins and of the sins of our nation as well. If we have offended someone we need to ask for their forgiveness and be willing to forgive others.

Returning to God is accompanied by a renewed commitment to follow his ways in his Word. Jewish people eat many sweet things including honey at the festive meal of the New Year to symbolise wanting the year ahead to be a sweet year. God's Word is often compared to the sweetness of honey.

We are reminded that the words and promises in the Bible bring blessings into our lives and will lead us in paths of righteousness,

How sweet are your words to my taste, sweeter than honey to my mouth. I gain understanding from your precepts: therefore I hate every wrong path. (Psalms 119:103-104)

The ordinances of the Lord are sure and altogether righteous. They are more precious than gold, than pure gold: they are sweeter than honey from the comb. (Psalms 19:9-10)

We return to God with the sweetness of following his Word and renewed fellowship with him.

Main Message

God set this holiday so people would turn back to him and focus on renewing their relationship with him. The Feast of Trumpets shows us how important it is to take time for our relationship with God to be restored, refreshed and strengthened.

It is good to repent and turn back to God at all times throughout the year but there is also something wonderful about starting a New Year fresh and close to God.

We enjoy the excitement of a New Year in our family and all that the coming year holds for us in our walk with God.

Prayer

Lord, thank you that we can confess our sins and return to a close relationship with you. We pray to value and enjoy a renewed relationship with you. We pray for our nation confessing the sins committed against you. Please forgive us and help us to return to your ways. Amen

The Feast of Trumpets – *Rosh Hashanah*

Chapter 5

The Day of Atonement
Yom Kippur

To the Lord our God belong compassion and forgiveness...
Daniel 9:9

He is the atoning sacrifice for our sins.
1 John 2:2

Introduction

The Day of Atonement is a day of fasting for all the people of Israel. It is called *Yom Kippur* and is the holiest holiday in the Hebrew calendar. *Kippur* in Hebrew means "atonement", to put something right through paying the penalty. The holiday takes place on the tenth day of the seventh month *Tishrei,* which usually occurs during the month of September or October. The fast begins in the evening after the ninth day and ends twenty-five hours later.

> *The tenth day of the seventh month is the Day of Atonement. Hold a sacred assembly and deny yourselves, and present a food offering to the Lord. Do not do any work on that day, because it is the Day*

> *of Atonement, when atonement is made for you before the Lord your God. (Leviticus 23:27-29)*

Yom Kippur concludes the period of seeking God in repentance. It started from the New Year and spans the ten days in between.

So much of the message and meaning of the Day of Atonement was fulfilled in Jesus and it is a representation of his divine purpose. Jesus fully understood the depth and purpose of atonement and the cost that was required of him to make atonement for the sins of the world.

The Biblical and historical background of the holiday

God gave instructions for the Day of Atonement, so that atonement would be made for sin and through this people could be forgiven.

> *...because on this day atonement will be made for you to cleanse you. Then before the Lord you will be clean of your sins...This is to be a lasting ordinance for you; Atonement is to be made once a year for all the sins of the Israelites. (Leviticus 16:30)*

On the Day of Atonement all the people of Israel were required to fast, abstaining from food, drink and work. It was a holy day, set apart to seek God's forgiveness because sin had separated them from God.

> *But your iniquities have separated you from your God; your sins have hidden his face from you, so that he will not hear. (Isaiah 59:2)*

There needed to be restitution to restore the relationship between God and the people of Israel. At the time of Temple worship, the priests were required to sacrifice animals as a sin offering on behalf of the people of Israel. The shedding of the blood and the life of the animal was made as the covering penalty for sin.

> *For the life of a creature is the blood, and I have given it to you to make atonement for yourselves on the altar; it is the blood that makes atonement for one's life. (Leviticus 17:11)*

Once a year the High priest would enter the Holy of Holies, behind the curtain, in the Temple, to make atonement for his sins and for the sins of Israel. He would enter the place where the Ark of the Covenant was in the sanctuary, the place where God's presence dwelt with his people Israel. He would bring the blood of the sacrificed animals in order to seek forgiveness for the sins of the people of Israel.

> *This is how Aaron is to enter the sanctuary area; with a young bull for a sin offering and a ram for a burnt offering…From the Israelite community he is to take two male goats for a sin offering and a ram for a burnt offering. Aaron is to offer the bull for his own sin offering to make atonement for himself and his household. Then he is to take the two goats and present them before the Lord at the entrance to the tent of meeting. He is to cast lots for the two goats – one lot for the Lord and the other for the scapegoat. Aaron shall bring the goat whose lot falls to the Lord and sacrifice it for a sin offering.*
> *(Leviticus 16:3,5-9)*

> *He shall slaughter the goat for the sin offering for the people and take its blood behind the curtain and do with it as he did the bull's blood. He shall sprinkle it on the atonement cover and in front of it. In this way*

he will make atonement for the most holy place because of the uncleanness and rebellion of the Israelites whatever sins have been.
(Leviticus 16:15-16)

Once the High Priest had made atonement in the Temple for himself and the people of Israel, he laid his hands on the head of the scapegoat and confessed the sins of Israel over it. The goat was then led out of the city walls and sent out into the desert to die, taking the sins of Israel away with it.

The goat will carry on itself all their sins to a remote place; and the man shall release it in the wilderness. (Leviticus 16:22)

God made provision for the people of Israel through this holiday to cover them and cleanse them from their sins so his relationship with them could continue.

...because on this day atonement will be made for you, to cleanse you. Then, before the Lord, you will be clean from all your sins. (Leviticus 16:30)

Lessons God taught through the holiday of the Day of Atonement

God's holiness

God revealed he is holy and sin cannot be permitted in his presence. He cannot abide with sin. Sin is consumed in God's holy presence, such as when Uzziah touched the Ark of the Covenant he died and the sons of Aaron died when they entered the Holy of Holies *(Leviticus 16:1)*. There needed to be a way made for man to be restored to a relationship with a holy God.

God is Just

God is just and will not let sin go without punishment. God gave a day of fasting every year when the whole nation of Israel had to address the seriousness of sin. Blood had to be shed to atone for sin and made a way for God's judgement to be attained. Through atonement God made a way to reconcile his relationship with people.

The way Jewish people celebrate the holiday of *Yom Kippur*

Jewish families gather for a pre-fast meal before the holiday. The meal should end one hour before sundown and all healthy adults fast. Boys from *Bar Mitzvah* (age thirteen) and girls from *Bat Mitzvah* (age twelve) fast. Women light the candles for the holiday and a memorial candle is lit for members of the family who have passed away. It is traditional to wear white clothes for purity. This is taken from the idea spoken about in Isaiah 1 that God makes sins whiter than snow through forgiveness. People also don't wear leather shoes, as a sign of humility. The fast means no food or drink or washing or sexual relations. Fasting is a way of acknowledging how dependent people are on God and in need of his help.

Religious Jewish people go to the Synagogue and hear the blowing of the *shofar*. Men wear their *Tallits,* their prayer shawls. There are five services during Yom Kippur. The service begins with *Kol Nidrei* on the eve of Yom Kippur which means "all vows", a prayer to absolve yourself of all vows and oaths you made in the previous year.

During the day there are several readings in the Synagogue about God's judgement for disobedience such as that of King Saul (*1 Samuel 15-1-34).* The book of Jonah is read which describes a people being saved after repentance. Remembering these events reveals that no one escapes God's judgement. God makes a way for people through atonement and forgiveness to be restored to a relationship with him. The role of the High Priest during the Temple times is also described during the Synagogue service. Bible readings about confessing the sins of the nation as well as individual sins are read,

If my people, who are called by my name, will humble themselves and pray and seek my face and turn from their wicked ways, then I will hear from heaven, and I will forgive their sin and will heal their land. (2 Chronicles 7:14)

Readings about God's comfort to those who are contrite in heart are also read,

Who is a God like you, who pardons sin and forgives the transgression of the remnant of his inheritance? You do not stay angry forever but delight to show mercy. (Micah 7:18)

In the evening, just before sundown on *Yom Kippur*, the *Neila* prayer is prayed. It is a prayer asking for one's name to be written into the Book of Life. It is believed the Gates of Mercy are closing towards the end of *Yom Kippur* and it is the last chance for one's name to be written in the Book of Life. It is prayed before the open ark in which the scrolls of scripture are kept. The service ends with the prayer *Shema*,

Hear, O Israel the Lord our God, the Lord is one. (Deuteronomy 6:4).

There is then a long blast of the *shofar,* representing the sound of redemption bringing the service to a close. People leave the Synagogue wishing one another a good New Year. People go home to eat a meal and it is traditional to put up the first post for the *sukkah* or booth ready for the next holiday which is the Feast of Tabernacles.

In Israel much of everyday life comes to a standstill on *Yom Kippur*. The traffic stops and people freely walk on the roads. Television and radio broadcasts cease. The whole country is affected as the nation stops to observe *Yom Kippur*. Most of the people fast on *Yom Kippur* as the nation come to a standstill in order to turn to God.

How the holiday relates to Jesus' ministry and teaching

Jesus made Atonement

God is holy and sin cannot dwell in his presence. The Bible is very clear that only the shedding of blood makes atonement for sin,

> *...without the shedding of blood there is no forgiveness. (Hebrews 9:22)*

> *For the life of a creature is in the blood, and I have given it to you to make atonement for yourselves on the altar; it is the blood that makes atonement for one's life. (Leviticus 17:11)*

Jesus' blood was shed and his death made atonement for all humanity's sin. Only through his atonement can people be cleansed from sin and enter into the presence of God to have fellowship with him.

> *God presented Christ as a sacrifice of atonement, through the shedding of blood to be received by faith. He did this to demonstrate his righteousness, because in his forbearance he had left the sins committed beforehand unpunished. (Romans 3:25)*

He is the atoning sacrifice for our sins, and not only ours but also the sins of the whole world. (1John 2:2)

Every year on the Day of Atonement animals had to be sacrificed to make atonement for the sins of the people of Israel. This was done as a covering until Jesus, the Lamb of God, was sacrificed,

Day after day every priest stands and performs his religious duties; again and again he offers the same sacrifices, which can never take away sins. But when this priest offered for all time one sacrifice, he sat down at the right hand of God. (Hebrews 10:11,12)

It is important to remember that Jesus did not abolish the law. The Bible says the law was a foreshadow of what Jesus would do.

The law is only a shadow of the good things coming not the realities themselves. (Hebrews 10:1)

Jesus said all things written about him in the scriptures must be fulfilled for God's plan to be achieved,

Everything must be fulfilled that is written about me in the Law of Moses, the Prophets and the Psalms. Then he opened their minds so they could understand the Scriptures. (Luke 24:44-45)

Isaiah prophesied that Jesus would take the punishment for the sin of the whole world,

But he was pierced for our transgressions, he was crushed for our iniquities; the punishment that brought us peace was on him...Yet it was the Lord's will to crush him and cause him to suffer, and though the Lord makes his life an offering for sin...my righteous servant will justify many, and he will bear their iniquities...For he bore the sin of many, and made intercession for the transgressors. (Isaiah 53:5,10-12)

God had a plan so that sin would no longer separate people from God and it was fulfilled by Jesus, it was prophesied in Psalm 40 that he would do this.

Therefore, when Christ came into the world, he said: "Sacrifice and offering you did not desire, but a body you prepared for me with burnt offerings and sin offerings you were not pleased. Then I said, 'Here I am – it is written about me in the scroll I have come to do your will, my God.'" (Hebrews 10:5-7, Psalms 40:6-8)

And by that will, we have been made holy through the sacrifice of the body of Jesus Christ. (Hebrews 10:10)

Jesus fulfilled the need for atonement once and for all, after his sacrifice there was no more need for atonement. God's judgement of sin was completed and finished in Jesus' blood and death.

He was sacrificed for their sins once for all when he offered himself. (Hebrews 7:27)

The atonement Jesus made for us demonstrates the love God has for people.

To him who loves us and has freed us from our sins by his blood. (Revelations 1:5)

Jesus the High priest

During Temple times the High priest was permitted to enter the Holy of Holies behind the curtain in the Temple once a year to sprinkle the blood on behalf of the people of Israel. Only the High priest was allowed on this day to enter the presence of God where the Ark of the Covenant and God's mercy seat were. The Bible says Jesus entered on our behalf and became High priest forever,

> *We have this hope as an anchor for the soul, firm and secure. It enters the inner sanctuary behind the curtain, where our forerunner, Jesus, has entered on our behalf. He has become a high priest forever, in the order of Melchizedek. (Hebrews 6:19-20)*

Which was prophesied he would do. *(Psalms 110:4).*

> *When Christ came as high priest of the good things that are now already here, he went through the greater and more perfect tabernacle that is not made with human hands, that is to say, is not a part of this creation. He did not enter by means of the blood of goats and calves; but he entered the Most Holy Place once for all by his own blood, thus obtaining eternal redemption. (Hebrews 9:11-12)*

After Jesus died, the Temple curtain was torn in two, from top to bottom, removing the separation of God's presence from people.

> *The curtain of the temple was torn in two from top to bottom. (Mark 15:38)*

Believers' names in the Book of life

Getting your name into the Book of Life is part of the prayers of *Yom Kippur*. The Book of Life is referred to in several places in the Bible; Daniel, Psalms, Luke, Philippians and Revelations. Believing in Jesus and his death that paid atonement for our sin ensures a person's name is written in the Book of Life. Jesus told his followers to,

> *"Rejoice that your names are written in heaven."*
> *(Luke 10:20)*

Followers of Jesus know their names are written in the Book of Life and they will be with him for all eternity,

> *I will never blot out the name of that person from the book of life, but will acknowledge that name before my Father and his angels. (Revelation 3:5)*

Those people whose names are not written in the Book of Life will be thrown into the lake of fire, and separated from God eternally.

> *Anyone whose name was not found written in the book of life was thrown into the lake of fire. (Revelation 20:15)*

The spiritual lessons of the holiday and how they apply to us today

The seriousness of sin

Sin separates us from God and God hates what sin does to us. It is so serious that Jesus had to come and shed his blood to die to make atonement for our sin. Seeking to keep sin out of our lives and follow God's way by his grace brings transformation and blessings to our lives.

God's forgiveness and covering

By Jesus making atonement and covering for our sin by his blood being shed and his death made the way for reconciliation with God. Our names are written in the Book of Life.

Fasting, individually and as a nation

Israel was given instructions to have a day of national fasting to restore their relationship with God. Fasting was something Jesus said his followers should do. It is a way of humbly turning to God and recognising our dependency on him both for our nation and our individual walk with him. A day of national fasting and taking time to confess the sins of our country is so powerful as a means of turning back to God and seeking God's will for the nation. It is also important that we take time to confess our sins in our own lives so we can walk closely with God.

The Day of Atonement was remembered by the early followers of Jesus and is mentioned in the New Testament. We know this as Paul referred to it on his boat journey and when he arrived at Lasea a town in the south of Crete,

> *Much time had been lost, and sailing had already become dangerous because by now it was after the Day of Atonement. (Acts 27:5)*

Many Messianic Jews and Christians fast on the Day of Atonement for the salvation of the people of Israel and other people so that they may know the Messiah who paid the penalty for sin.

Main message

As believers, we deeply value and understand the spiritual significance of the Day of Atonement and all it means to us. There was no other way for us to be in a relationship with God except through Jesus and the atoning sacrifice he made for us.

Yom Kippur, the Day of Atonement in Israel, was a special experience for us. It was wonderful to watch a nation come to a standstill all together and to know the reason they do this is because God set a day to stop and acknowledge the need for atonement.

Prayer

Thank you, Jesus, for making atonement for us and that you are our High Priest. We pray to walk closely with you and confess our sins and the sins of our nation. We pray for the spiritual veil to be removed from the people of Israel as well as other nations so many will know you as Saviour. Amen.

Chapter 6

The Feast of Tabernacles
Sukkot

*He who believes in me – from his innermost being will flow
rivers of living water.*
John 7:38

Introduction

The holiday of the Feast of Tabernacles celebrates the time
when the people of Israel lived in tabernacles in the desert on
their way to Israel. Living in temporary shelters they depended
on God for all their needs in the desert, having left Egypt. The
Hebrew name for the holiday is *Sukkot* which means
tabernacles. The tabernacle is a symbol of God's presence and
protection.

> *On the fifteenth day of the seventh month the Lord's
> Festival of Tabernacles begins, and it lasts for seven
> days...for seven days present food offering to the
> Lord. So beginning with the fifteenth day of the
> seventh month, after you have gathered the crops of
> the land, celebrate the festival to the Lord...the first
> day is a day of Sabbath rest, and the eighth day also
> is a day of Sabbath rest.*

On the first day you are to take branches from luxuriant trees – from palms, willows and other leafy trees – and rejoice before the Lord your God for seven days.

Live in temporary shelters for seven days: All native-born Israelites are to live in such shelters so your descendants will know that I had the Israelites live in temporary shelters when I brought them out of Egypt. I am the Lord your God.
(Leviticus 23:34, 36,39,40, 42-43)

The holiday is celebrated from the 15th to the 22nd of the month of *Tishrei*, the seventh month in the Hebrew calendar, around October. The holiday takes place after the gathering of the autumn harvest and is also called Holiday of Ingathering, *Hag ha Asif*. Thanksgiving for the autumn harvest is a part of the holiday. Another Hebrew name is *Zman Simchatenu* which means time of our rejoicing based on the verse in Leviticus 23:40,

"...rejoice before the Lord your God for seven days."

The Feast of Tabernacles is referred to in Exodus, Leviticus, Deuteronomy, Numbers, Ezra, Nehemiah and John. The holiday lasts for seven days and then the next day the eighth day is also a day of rest.

Sukkot, the Feast of Tabernacles, was one of the three annual pilgrimage festivals when the people of Israel were required to go to Jerusalem to worship God at the Temple and celebrate there.

Jesus taught and revealed amazing spiritual truths at the Feast of Tabernacles in Jerusalem which can be fully appreciated in the context of the holiday celebrations.

The Biblical and historical background of the holiday

During *Sukkot*, God instructed the people of Israel to live in temporary shelters for seven days to remind them of the temporary dwellings they had lived in while in the desert and to tell their children what God had done for them on their way to Israel,

> *This is to be a lasting ordinance for the generations to come; celebrate it in the seventh month. Live in temporary shelters for seven days. (Leviticus 23:41)*

The holiday was also a time to celebrate in gratitude to God for the blessing of the autumn harvest. The autumn crops included wheat, figs, dates, pomegranates, olives and grapes.

> *Celebrate the Festival of Ingathering at the end of the year, when you gather in your crops from the field. (Exodus 23:16)*

During the holiday the people of Israel were instructed "to rejoice before the Lord". The Bible describes putting branches from several trees together as part of rejoicing and worshipping God.

> *On the first day you are to take branches from luxuriant trees – from palms, willows and other leafy trees – and rejoice before the Lord your God for seven days. (Leviticus 23:40)*

Date palm, myrtle and willow branches were bunched together and held in one hand, they are called *lulav* in Hebrew, and a citrus fruit with a lemon fragrance, an *etrog,* is held in the other hand. Together these are known as the four species and were waved in the Temple courtyard as part of worship to God. Sacrifices were made to the Lord each day as well.

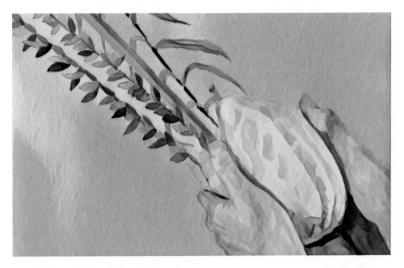

At the Temple in Jerusalem a water ceremony took place during *Sukkot* called *Simchat Beit ha Sho'eva.* Each morning, the priests would go to the pool of Siloam near Jerusalem with golden containers and fill them with fresh water. As the priests brought the water to the Temple there was much rejoicing, singing praises to God. The priests poured the water from the golden containers on the altar, at the same time wine was poured too and they circled around the altar. When water was poured the *shofar,* a ram's horn was blown. People sang Psalms and waved the tree branches, the *lulav* with the citrus fruit, *etrog.* There was dancing as well as playing instruments all in worship to God at this ceremony. At night time candles were lit and people carried torches.

The pouring of the water had a special spiritual meaning, expressing dependence on God for salvation and for the cleansing from sin.

It was a very special ceremony which took place every day with the culmination and high point of the holiday taking place on the seventh day and last day called *Hoshana raba,* which means Great Salvation. The priests poured the water and circled the altar seven times as the people cried out to God for salvation, calling *Hoshana* "save us".

After all the water ceremonies had taken place on the eighth day there was a Holy assembly which is called *Shemini Atzeret*. No one worked on this day and spent another day in devotion to God.

> *Celebrate the festival... the first day is a day of Sabbath rest, and the eighth day also is a day of Sabbath rest. (Leviticus 23:39)*

Lessons God taught through the holiday of the Feast of Tabernacles

Depending on God

God provided for all the needs of the people of Israel while they were in the desert. They were exposed and vulnerable, dependent on him for everything. They needed food and water each day, as well as their clothing and shoes lasting. They relied on him for shelter in their tabernacles. God also provided protection from the surrounding nations who sought to attack them. During these circumstances, they came under the shelter and protection of the Most High learning they could trust God to take care of his people.

Remembering God's provision and protection for his people

These lessons, which God taught the first generation of the people of Israel who left Egypt, were to be remembered by all future generations as valuable lessons. In the Bible they were instructed to dwell in a *Sukkah* during the holiday, to remind them of the experience their ancestors had in the desert. Recalling what God had done in the past was an important way of building faith to trust God in the future with the challenges that they would face. All generations were to experience spending time in temporary booths, exposed to nature, to remember and value their dependency on God.

Thankfulness to God

The holiday was a time to be grateful and celebrate all God had done for his people. They were grateful for his provision and protection in the desert and also for him providing the land of Israel to live in and blessing the harvest.

> For seven days celebrate the festival to the LORD your God at the place the LORD will choose. For the LORD your God will bless you in all your harvest and in all the work of your hands, and your joy will be complete. (Deuteronomy 16:15)

Thanksgiving to God was displayed in public celebrations at the Temple with the waving of branches and the citrus fruit, as described in Leviticus. God showed that it is important to take time to appreciate what he has done and continues to do for his people.

The setting of the holiday

Sukkot and rejoicing in the Lord followed the holidays of New Year, *Rosh Hashanah* and the Day of Atonement, *Yom Kippur*. The focus of the two earlier holidays was repentance, fasting and returning to God which led to rejoicing and being thankful to God in *Sukkot* having returned to a right relationship with God.

Prophetic words connected to the holiday

The Feast of Tabernacles also holds a prophetic message for all people. It reveals that a time will come when all nations will worship the Lord as king over all the earth during the holiday.

Then the survivors from all the nations that have attacked Jerusalem will go up year after year to worship the King, the Lord Almighty, and to celebrate the Festival of Tabernacles. If any of the peoples of the earth do not go up to Jerusalem to worship the King, the Lord Almighty, they will have no rain. (Zechariah 14:16)

The way Jewish people celebrate the holiday of the Feast of Tabernacles

The Sukkah

God told the people of Israel to dwell in *sukkahs*, temporary booths during the holiday. It is customary for Jewish people to set up the first piece of the structure of the *sukkah* at the end of the previous holiday of *Yom Kippur*. People believe God provided spiritual covering through atonement for his people at *Yom Kippur* and he also provided for their physical needs at *Sukkot*. Both spiritual and physical needs are given by God and appreciated in these holidays.

The *sukkah* must have three sides with one side open. It can be attached to a permanent structure but cannot be built under a roof or tree. The roof is made of palms, pine or olive branches and must be loosely arranged so as to be able to see the stars at night through the branches. Children take part in the building of the *sukkah* and decorate it inside with flowers or displays of fruit and vegetables, a reminder of God's provision of the harvest.

Spending time in the *sukkah* is an important part of the holiday, whether it is having meals there or sleeping in the *sukkah*, looking up to the night sky. It is a time to think about the experience of their ancestors living in *sukkahs* in the desert. Some also study and discuss the Bible in their *sukkah*. It is also a time to get back to nature and a time to live without all the material comforts of modern living. To think about what are the essentials of life, knowing being in a *sukkah* is just temporary but the permanent structure of home is still there.

All Jewish people, regardless of wealth and background, are required to live in a *sukkah,* reminding people of the sense of equality in the Lord's eyes. The structure is taken down each year at the end of the holiday.

Ushpizin

It is traditional for Jewish people to talk about their Biblical ancestors in the *sukkah* and they call them *ushpizim*, which is an Aramaic word meaning guests. Stories about people from the Bible are told and their influence in history is discussed. For example there are seven guests known as the seven fathers of Israel who made a journey during their lifetime, just as the people of Israel had to make the journey through the desert to the land of Israel.

Abraham, who was the first forefather of Israel, left his country of birth and moved to Canaan; Isaac never left Canaan but moved from place to place within Canaan; Jacob left Canaan to move to Egypt towards the end of his life; Joseph who was sold by his brothers moved to Egypt; Moses wandered in the desert for forty years; Aaron who was the head of the priests spent forty years in the desert. David who was pursued by Saul, escaped to the land of the Philistines.

During the holiday people talk about these men in the Bible as well as seven women thought of as the mothers of Israel; Sarah, Rebecca, Rachel, Leah, Miriam, Hannah and Deborah. They discuss their contribution to faith, their character and the attributes they brought, such as righteousness, bravery, perseverance and wisdom. All these people followed God and his plan for their lives and though they made mistakes and failed at times, they grew from these mistakes and did great things for the Lord during their lifetime.

Maimonides, the Jewish scholar, believed Jewish people have been inspired by the character of these men and women, influencing many and helping them to endure persecution throughout history and remain faithful to God.

The Four Species

The Bible describes putting branches from several trees together as part of the worship to God during the holiday. These branches, *lulav* and the citrus fruit, the *etrog* were waved before the Lord in the Temple courtyard. These days they are waved by the Western Wall of the Temple in Israel and in synagogues every day during *Sukkot* whilst praying in each direction of the four corners of the world, to honour God as ruler over all the world.

A famous folk story is told at *Sukkot* about a village called *Helem*, a place famed for its foolish people. Two men who lived there did not have enough money to buy a *lulav* and an *etrog*, so they put their money together to buy them. As soon as they had bought them, they began to argue about who would have the honour of saying the first blessing. The Rabbi, who was the only wise man in the village, told them to stop arguing and that he would settle the matter. He took the *etrog* and cut it in half. The two men were shocked because the *etrog* was now useless and nobody would get to say the blessing.

The Rabbi told them to throw it away saying, "Even if it were whole, what good would your blessing be if it came from an angry and a jealous heart? Even the most perfect *etrog* would be useless if the blessing did not come from a right heart."

The Water ceremonies

In the Synagogue people encircle the ark, the place where the Torah scroll is kept. This represents the circling around the altar in the Temple courtyard at the water ceremonies. Prayers are said called *Hoshanot*, which are pleas for salvation and the four species are held. On the final day of *Sukkot* which is the *Hoshana Raba*, the great *Hosanna*, the ark is circled seven times with an additional final prayer for salvation.

Bible Passages

The book of Ecclesiastes is read in the Synagogue on the *Shabbat* during *Sukkot*, in this passage King Solomon questioned the meaning of life, and came to the conclusion;

> *What does man gain from all his labour at which he toils under the sun? (Ecclesiastes 1:3)*

> *...here is the conclusion of the matter: Fear God and keep his commandments, for this is the duty of all mankind. (Ecclesiastes 12:13)*

The *Hallel* is said which is *Psalms 113-118* and within *Psalm 118:25* the prayer is *"Lord save us"*. Zechariah 14 is read, the prophecy when people from all the nations will worship God at the Feast of Tabernacles.

In Israel the priests gather together at the Western Wall *(Kotel)* at the holiday to say the Aaronic blessing called *Birkat Cohanim* over the people of Israel. This has become a special event of the holiday and many people enjoy going to witness this in Jerusalem,

> *The LORD bless you and keep you; the LORD make his face shine on you and be gracious to you; the LORD turn his face towards you and give you peace. (Numbers 6:24)*

The eighth day, the day immediately after the holiday, is known as *Shemini Atzert*. Jewish people believe God wanted to spend one more day with his people after the holiday of *Sukkot* before they go back to their busy routines of everyday life and is considered a joyful time spending another day with God. On this day they also start praying for rain for the coming year.

The day after the holiday of *Sukkot* in the Hebrew calendar is also called *Simchat Torah*, which means rejoicing over the *Torah*. *Simchat Torah* is not mentioned in the Bible. It is a holiday that began around 1000 AD celebrating the completion of reading the *Torah* and showing reverence for God's Word. Once the last portion of Deuteronomy is read in the Synagogue, the reading goes back to the start of Genesis demonstrating the study of God's Word has no end.

The blessing of studying God's Word is recognised as there is always something new to learn, with fresh revelation in his Word. The *Torah* scrolls are taken out of the Ark where they are kept and people dance holding the *Torah* scrolls and children wave flags.

How the holiday relates to Jesus' teaching and ministry

Sukkot was one of the three pilgrimage festivals when Jewish people were required to be in Jerusalem. Jesus would have spent *Sukkot* in Jerusalem. It was important for Jesus to be there as he taught in the Temple courts giving incredible revelation about himself during the ceremonies and celebrations of the holiday.

> *Not until halfway through the festival did Jesus go up to the temple courts and begin to teach. The*

Jews there were amazed and asked, "How did this man get such learning without having been taught?" Jesus answered, "My teaching is not my own. It comes from the one who sent me."
(John 7:14-16)

Jesus offered living water at Sukkot: salvation and the Holy Spirit

For six days water ceremonies took place when the priests poured water on the altar called *Simchat Beit ha sho'eva*. On the seventh day, which was the high point of the water ceremony and the most significant day of the holiday called the great Salvation, (*Hoshanna raba*), the people were crying out to God, praying "save us". Jesus stood up at this moment on that important day and declared in a loud voice that he provides the salvation they were praying for.

On the last and greatest day of the festival, Jesus stood and said in a loud voice, "Let anyone who is thirsty come to me and drink. Whoever believes in me, as Scripture has said, rivers of living water will flow from within them." By this he meant the Spirit, whom those who believed in him were later to receive. Up to that time the Spirit had not been given, since Jesus had not yet been glorified. On hearing his words, some of the people said, "Surely this man the Prophet." Others said, "He is the Messiah." (John 7:37-41)

Jesus' name *Yeshua* means salvation and he directly responded to their plea for salvation. He said anyone who believed in him would receive the living water of the Holy Spirit. The prayers of *Sukkot* and the meaning of water ceremonies were fulfilled in Jesus on that day in *Sukkot* and God answered their prayers during this holiday.

The spiritual lessons of the holiday and how they apply to us today

Jesus gives all of us living water

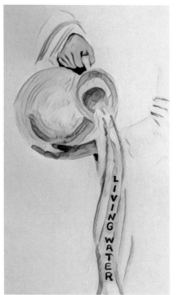

At the high point of the water pouring ceremony and the most important day of the *Sukkot*, Jesus offered living water. His offer of living water still stands today for anyone who would come to him and believe in him.

"Whoever drinks the water I give them will never thirst. Indeed, the water I give them will become in them a spring of water welling up to eternal life." (John 4:14)

Only through Jesus can we receive living waters to satisfy our souls and receive salvation.

Come, all you who are thirsty, come to the waters. (Isaiah.55:1)

With joy you will draw water from the wells of salvation of living water. (Isaiah 12:3)

Let the one who is thirsty come; and let the one who wishes take the free gift of the water of life. (Revelation 22:17)

The living water that Jesus is talking about is not only salvation but also a relationship with him, as the Holy Spirit lives in us and will sustain us throughout our lives.

> *The LORD will guide you always; he will satisfy your needs in a sun-scorched land and will strengthen your frame. You will be like a well-watered garden, like a spring whose waters never fail. (Isaiah 58:11)*

> *It is the Spirit who gives life. (John 6:63)*

God actually warns of the dangers of turning away from him and tells of the living water he provides in a relationship with him,

> *My people have committed two sins: They have forsaken me, the spring of living water, and have dug their own cisterns, broken cisterns that cannot hold water. (Jeremiah 2:13)*

> *Those who turn away from you will be written in the dust – because they have forsaken the LORD, the spring of living water. (Jeremiah 17:13)*

Sukkot reminds us of our dependency on God

The holiday of *Sukkot* reminds us of God's promise to provide for us and protect us, especially in vulnerable circumstances, just as the people of Israel in the desert were dependent him. God demonstrated he would provide for his people no matter what the circumstance were, and it is an important message given to all his people who believe in him.

We cannot control nature, nor can we control all the circumstances in our lives, but we do have the assurance that God is in control. He will take care of us and we can trust him. Sometimes we are in vulnerable situations and God shows how much he will take care of us during those times. We learn to

114

rely on him at a deeper level than if we had always been in secure surroundings.

> *And my God will meet all your needs according to his glory in Christ Jesus. (Philippians 4:19)*

God will be with us in every circumstance. The word Tabernacle actually means to dwell with and the Bible says,

> *How lovely is your dwelling place,*
> *O LORD Almighty! (Psalm 84:1)*

God dwelt with his people in the desert, never leaving them even once. He draws close to us, dwelling with us in all circumstances and we know his presence is always with us.

> *Whoever dwells in the shelter of the Most High will rest in the shadow of the Almighty. (Psalm 91:1)*

> *And in him you too are being built together to become a dwelling in which God lives by his Spirit. (Ephesians 2:22)*

Sukkahs are temporary dwellings; our everlasting home is in heaven

Living in a temporary shelter is part of the holiday, with the message of dependency on God, but there is also another message which it is important to recognise – that our lives here on earth are temporary and our true everlasting home is with him in heaven.

The book of Ecclesiastes is read during *Sukkot* and teaches us that our time on earth is temporary and that generations will come and go *(Ecclesiastes 1:4.)* Jesus spoke about the permanent homes he has prepared for us in heaven. Passages in John and 2 Corinthians confirm this truth that our homes on earth are temporary and our eternal home is in heaven.

My Father's house has many rooms; if that were not so, would I have told you that I am going there to prepare a place for you? (John 14:2)

For we know that if the earthly tent we live in is destroyed, we have a building from God, an eternal house in heaven, not built by human hands. (2 Corinthians 5:1)

A Holiday of Ingathering – a harvest of souls

The holiday is also called the Festival of Ingathering, *Hag ha Asif*. Part of the prophetic message of *Sukkot* is about people from every nation worshipping God and that there will be a full ingathering of people from all nations coming into his kingdom. During Temple times sacrifices were made on behalf of the nations for people to know God. In the New Testament the message of the Gospel going worldwide to all peoples is given. People from all over the world worship and follow Jesus and we look forward to a great harvest and ingathering of souls from every nation. It also reminds us of Christ's millennial reign when he shall rule from Jerusalem *(Revelation 20)*.

Each of the three pilgrimage holidays, *Pesach, Shavuot, Sukkot*, required the Jewish people to go up to Jerusalem. Each of these holidays represent a significant spiritual event of God's plan revealed to mankind in his Word. *Pesach –* Passover with the death of Jesus as the sacrificial Passover Lamb making a way for the forgiveness of sin and a restored relationship to God. *Shavuot –* Pentecost with the coming of the Holy Spirit so people can lead lives following God, have both been fulfilled.

The only pilgrimage holiday that has not yet been fulfilled is *Sukkot*. The Feast of Tabernacles prophesies the full ingathering of souls from all nations worshipping God. This is significant and something about which we should have knowledge in order to pray for the full meaning of this holiday to come to pass, in the way the other two have been fulfilled.

There are already signs of this future promise as every year Christians from all over the world gather in Jerusalem for an event during the Feast of Tabernacles to worship the Lord. This event is organised by the Christian Embassy in Jerusalem.

Main Message

Sukkot shows us that our faith is strengthened by remembering what God has already done for us in our lives, we learn through these experiences that we can depend on God in all situations. Part of God's love for us is the promise to never leave us or forsake us. He will be with us and provide for us in all circumstances. The holiday reminds us of the salvation Jesus has given us and the streams of living water flowing through us so we will never thirst again.

We really liked going to Jerusalem for the Feast of Tabernacles celebrations. It was good to see Christians from so many different nations coming to praise and worship God together in Jerusalem. The atmosphere was very special and made us think of what is still to come in the future. It was lovely to see how the local people who live in Jerusalem enjoyed Christians coming from all over the world and the encouragement they bring. We also enjoyed meeting in a *sukkah* during the holiday with other believers in Israel to study the Word of God and share a meal together.

Prayer

Lord, we thank you for providing us with salvation and the Living Water that never runs dry. Thank you for your presence in our lives and provision for us especially in hard circumstances. We pray for the ingathering harvest of all your people from every nation. Amen.

The Feast of Tabernacles – *Sukkot*

Chapter 7

The Feast of Lots
Purim

For such a time as this.
Esther 4:14

Introduction

The holiday of *Purim* celebrates the events described in the book of Esther in the Bible. It is an interesting holiday because God is not actually mentioned in Esther. However, God's sovereignty is clearly demonstrated throughout the book and it is a joyous and valuable festival. The holiday of *Purim* has been celebrated by the Jewish people ever since the events that took place in the book of Esther in the fifth century BC. It is therefore a festival that started being celebrated after the other holidays given in the Bible and is different to the other biblical holidays in this aspect.

Purim is celebrated on the 14th of *Adar*, the twelfth month in the Hebrew calendar, around the end of February or beginning of March. The word *Purim* means "Lots" as lots were cast during the story of Esther.

The book of John tells us that Jesus was in Jerusalem for a Feast of the Jews *(John 5:1)*. The Feast being referred to is very likely *Purim* as the next holiday John wrote about was Passover and *Purim* precedes Passover in the Hebrew calendar.

Biblical and historical background of the holiday

The book of Esther is set in the time of the Persian Empire (539-330 BC). The holiday does not have instructions the way other biblical holidays have and it is worthwhile looking at the story of Esther.

The people of Israel had been taken into exile by King Nebuchadnezzar of Babylon in approximately 598 BC until King Cyrus permitted them to leave in 538 BC. Many Jewish people returned to the land of Israel, however a large Jewish community remained behind, including Esther, who lived in the citadel of Susa. King Ahasuerus ruled over the Empire. His Greek title was Xerxes and during the third year of his reign, he held a banquet to display his power and wealth to his military leaders and nobles from the one hundred and twenty-seven provinces under his rule from India to Egypt. The banquet took place in the citadel of Susa and during the occasion King Xerxes commanded his wife Queen Vashti, the granddaughter of Nebuchadnezzar, to come to the banquet. Queen Vashti refused, and King Xerxes dethroned her for the disrespect she showed to him and the influence it would have on other women in the Empire.

King Xerxes then set about finding a new queen. Women were brought from all over the King's realm, including Esther. Esther won favour with all the people around her and King Xerxes chose her to be his new wife. Her Persian name Esther means "star" and her Hebrew name was *Hadassah* which means "myrtle". When she was selected, Mordecai, told her to keep her Jewish identity hidden. He was her guardian and cousin and had raised her since her parents died.

Mordecai was an official in the court of Susa, and also a prominent leader amongst the Jewish people. When Mordecai overheard a plot to kill the King by two eunuchs called Bigathana and Teresh, he told Queen Esther. She informed King Xerxes and he had them hung. This was recorded in the King's Book of Annals.

King Xerxes appointed an adviser called Haman to be one of his chief advisers. He had Haman ride through the streets of Susa to show that he had been promoted, so people would recognise his new appointment. People were expected to kneel down to the newly appointed adviser. All the people knelt to Haman except Mordecai, who refused to kneel to him and pay homage to him, as it was idolatrous to kneel to any man as a god.

Haman's anger burned against Mordecai and he determined to get rid not only of Mordecai but all the Jewish people in the Empire. Haman was a descendant of the Amalekites, who were the first nation to attack the people of Israel on their way to the Promised Land, an enemy whom the people of Israel under Moses fought against. Later on in history God instructed King Saul to destroy them, but King Saul disobeyed God *(1 Samuel 15.)* The result of King Saul's disobedience was that the Amalekite people continued to exist, and Haman was one of their descendants. He hated the Jewish people in the same way his ancestors had done and sought their destruction.

Haman decided on a massacre. He cast lots *(Purim)* to choose which day to destroy the Jewish people and it fell on the 13th day of *Adar*. He also had special gallows made on which to hang Mordecai. Haman turned King Xerxes against the Jewish people saying they did not obey the king's laws and the king would be better off without them because they were disloyal, and their customs were different. The King gave Haman permission to do as he pleased with the Jewish people.

When an edict of Haman's plans was issued in the citadel of Susa, Mordecai tore his clothes and started to wail. Esther's maids reported this to her and she sent one of her eunuchs to find out why he was so upset. Mordecai gave a copy of the edict for Esther to read and told her to beg the King for mercy. Esther responded that she could not approach the King without being summoned or she would be killed. To which Mordecai replied,

> *"Do not think that because you are in the king's house you alone of all the Jews will escape. For if you remain silent at this time, relief and deliverance for the Jews will arise from another place, but you and your father's family will perish. And who knows but that you have come to your royal position for such a time as this?" (Esther 4:13-14)*

Esther sent a message back to Mordecai to gather all the Jewish community in Susa to fast for three days and that she and her maids would fast as well.

Esther said it was only after the fasting that she would approach the king.

> *"When this is done, I will go to the King, even though it is against the law. And if I perish, I will perish."*
> *(Esther 4:16)*

After fasting, Esther approached the King and he was pleased to see her, he extended his sceptre to her asking what her request was. She requested a banquet with the King and Haman. At this banquet Esther requested another banquet the following night with Haman and the king.

Haman was delighted and went about boasting of his favour with the Queen, as he alone was invited with the king. That night the King could not sleep and while he was awake he ordered the Book of Annals to be read to him. He then learned of how Mordecai had saved his life by exposing the plot to kill him. He found that Mordecai had not been rewarded for doing this. The next day he ordered Haman to fetch Mordecai to have him honoured with the royal robe and lead him through the city streets proclaiming what Mordecai had done to save the king.

That evening at the banquet the King again asked Esther what her request was, and she said,

> *"If I have found favour with you, O King, and if it pleases your majesty, grant me my life – this is my petition. And spare my people – for I and my people have been sold for destruction and slaughter and annihilation." (Esther 7:3,4)*

Esther then revealed to the King that it was Haman who had planned to massacre all the Jewish people.

> *"The adversary and enemy is this vile Haman." (Esther 7:6)*

Haman fell onto Esther, begging for his life, making the King even more incensed thinking Haman was molesting his wife. A eunuch informed the King that Haman had gallows at his house ready to use to hang Mordecai. The King ordered

Haman to be hung on them instead. He gave Haman's estate to Esther, which she gave to Mordecai, and Mordecai was raised to second in rank to the King.

The King also decreed that the Jews were to defend themselves against anyone who attacked them. Esther requested that Haman's ten sons also be hung on the gallows.

The Bible tells us,

> *But now the tables were turned and the Jews got the upper hand over those who hated them…the evil scheme Haman had devised against the Jews should come back on to his own head, and that he and his sons should be hanged on the gallows. (Esther 9:1,25)*

Mordecai recorded the event and declared the Jewish people were to celebrate every year in *Adar* on the 14th day to remember and celebrate what had taken place,

> *…the time when the Jews got relief from their enemies, and as the month when their sorrow was turned into joy and their mourning into a day of celebration. He wrote to them to observe the days as days of feasting and joy and giving presents of food to one another and gifts to the poor.*
> *(Esther 9:22)*

The holiday of *Purim* celebrates victory over evil as God delivered and defended the Jewish people.

Lessons God taught his people through the holiday of *Purim*

God protects his people

God showed the people of Israel that he was protecting them when they faced a desperate situation. He knew what was being planned against them and came to their rescue, turning the tables on the oppressor even whilst in exile.

God puts people into position and places of influence to serve him

Both Mordecai and Esther were used in the King's court to influence the King to save the Jewish people from death. Esther, as Queen, was able to go to the King, Mordecai told her that she was in her special position for this time.

> *"And who knows if you have come to the royal place for such a time as this." (Esther 4:14)*

Mordecai was a descendant of King Saul from the tribe of Benjamin. God had raised up someone from King Saul's line to destroy Haman and his sons, who were descendants of the Amalekites.

God hears and responds to the prayers and fasting of his people

The importance of fasting and prayer, especially as a community, is shown through the story of Esther. She declared a three day fast for all the Jewish community to humble themselves asking for God's help. It was not a coincidence that when the Jewish people were fasting, King Xerxes woke in the night and read the Annals of the King and found out that

Mordecai had saved his life, thus bringing favour to Mordecai. God was intervening on behalf of his people, so they would be victorious over evil.

God honoured Esther's obedience

Esther was willing to put her life into God's hands taking a risk at such an important time saying,

> "If I perish, I will perish." (Esther 4:16)

The way Jewish people celebrate the holiday of *Purim*

During *Purim,* the book of Esther *(Megillat Esther)* is read and people cheer when Mordecai's name is read. Everyone boos and stamps their feet when Haman's name is read using noise makers to block out the mention of his name.

On the Shabbat before *Purim*, the Bible portion about the Amalekites and their wickedness in trying to destroy the Jewish people is read. The day before *Purim,* Jewish people fast which is called the Fast of Esther.

There is much celebration, giving thanks for God's deliverance of the Jewish people. The holiday is a reminder that throughout history, people have tried to persecute and destroy them. The story of Esther gives hope and reaffirms God's protection for the Jewish people.

Gifts are given to the poor, so nobody is left out of the celebrations and gifts are given to friends as well. There is a festive meal to celebrate with family and friends. *Oznei Haman,* which means Haman ears, are three cornered pastries filled with sweetened poppy seeds which are eaten. People dress up in costumes and have parades. It is a time to celebrate and be joyful celebrating God's deliverance, remembering it was a time when sorrow was turned into joy.

How the holiday relates to Jesus' teaching and ministry

Jesus would have celebrated the holiday of *Purim* each year. Jewish people were required to celebrate the holiday since the events of *Purim* in the fifth century BC *(Esther 9:22)*. It was therefore a long-established part of the Hebrew calendar by the time Jesus was living in Israel.

Some scholars say the Festival of the Jews mentioned in John *(John 5:1)* was *Purim* because in the following chapter of John it says the Passover was near and *Purim* comes before Passover.

In the account of John where it mentions the Feast of the Jews it says that Jesus was near the sheep gate by the pool of Bethsaida and that it was Shabbat. A man was there who had been an invalid for thirty-eight years and Jesus healed him, giving an incredible gift of healing during this holiday.

Jesus was healing when it was the Shabbat and a holiday demonstrating God's love and concern for people disregarding religious rules. He said,

> *"My father is at work to this very day and I too am working." (John: 5:17)*

He called God his father, revealing who he was as well as the authority God had given him.

The spiritual lessons of the holiday and how they apply to us today

God puts people in place to fulfil his purposes

Esther and Mordecai were put in positions of influence. Throughout history God has been putting people in places and positions of influence for his purposes. God continues to raise up people for specific times and put them in strategic places for the role he has planned for them so his will is done. In the story of Esther, political power was taken away from an evil person and godly values were restored through a different person. We need to pray for God's people to be in the key positions that God has planned them for.

Following God's plans for each one of us

If we don't follow God's will and plan for us he will raise up someone else to fulfil his plans. Mordecai warned Esther if she did not act, deliverance would come from somewhere else. Esther showed incredible faith and courage knowing she might die but she chose to put her life in God's hands instead of trying to ensure her own safety. We may have to stand against evil for God's righteousness. God uses people in a powerful way who humbly submit to his will to do his work. Esther set a remarkable example for us to be inspired by and to follow.

Obedience to God's instructions

King Saul did not obey God's instruction to destroy the Amalekites with the result that their wickedness remained in their descendants who continued to seek the destruction of the Jewish people. God used a descendant of King Saul to correct his disobedience. This shows that if we don't stand up to evil and do what God tells us to do, there will be consequences for future generations. Our actions will affect generations to come and what we pass on will have impact.

Standing against anti-Semitism and Satan's plans

Haman was offended by Mordecai and instead of just turning against Mordecai, he decided to take his hatred out on all Jews. Haman is an example of an anti-Semitic person in history and there have been many people and political leaders through the years who have tried to destroy the Jewish people. The origins of anti-Semitism are from Satan and his hatred for the people whom God chose and used to bring salvation to the world through the Messiah *(John 4:22.)* Satan continues to hate the Jewish people because of God's plans and purposes for them described in Biblical Prophecy.

Christians should recognise the spiritual battle against the Jewish people and stand against anti-Semitism. Anti-Semitism has not gone away after the Holocaust and it is trying to re-establish its hatred again in society in many spheres in our day.

God's protection of the Jewish people

Purim reminds us of God's triumph over evil, protecting his people. God shows his faithfulness and commitment to his promises, written in his Word concerning the Jewish people. We need to know what his will is in his Word for them.

Prayer for Israel

Esther prayed and fasted for her people and she told her community to do the same. We too can pray and there are many Prayer for Israel groups worldwide that have recognised the need to pray for Israel in accordance with God's Word.

Praying and fasting for our own nation

Just as Esther recognised the need to turn to God in prayer for her people, we should pray and fast for our own nation, humbly asking for God's help in our country. There is power when believers unite in praying and fasting for God's help and intervention in the nation. We must seek his help to set us free from the enemy's strategy against our country.

Main message

Purim shows us the importance of turning to God for help when facing evil and through him victory over evil is possible. We can seek him in prayer and fasting and pray that God will give us the courage to take our stand for him when we need to.

We enjoyed reading the story of Esther during *Purim*. Messianic believers in Israel also like dressing up and celebrating *Purim* and God's deliverance.

Prayer

Lord, we thank you for your faithfulness and victory over evil. We pray you give us the courage to stand for you and use us in the places and times you have appointed for us. We pray your divine protection over our nation and Israel. Amen.

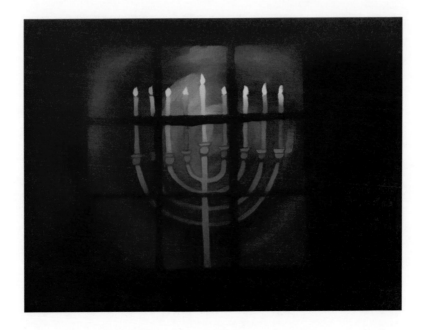

Chapter 8

The Feast of Dedication
Hanukkah

"I am the light of the world."
John 8:12

Introduction

The word *Hanukkah* means dedication. The holiday of the
Feast of Dedication celebrates the rededication of the Temple
to God in Jerusalem and the miracle that took place at that
time. It is also called the Feast of Lights, *Hag ha Orot* in
Hebrew. Both dedication and light are themes in the holiday.

Hanukkah takes place during the winter time on the 25th of
Kislev, which is the ninth month in the Hebrew calendar and
falls in late November or early December. The holiday lasts for
eight days.

The miracle occurred during the time between the Old
Testament and New Testament writers. Even though the
writing of God's Word was quiet at this time, God was still
showing his power and his intervention in the lives of his
people.

Even though the holiday of *Hanukkah* is not one of the Biblical Holidays, it is celebrated by the people of Israel as a valuable holiday because of what God did at that time. As believers in the Messiah, we recognise it as the Feast of Dedication referred to in the book of John, where it speaks about Jesus being in Jerusalem for the Feast of Dedication *(John 10:22)*. It is an interesting holiday to learn about.

The historical background to the holiday

The story of *Hanukkah* took place at a time when the Greek Empire dominated parts of the Middle East and other territories. Alexander the fourth ruled over the Empire from 175-163 BC and the Greek leaders were seeking to Hellenise the lands they had conquered. When Alexander died the Empire was split into four divisions. King Antiochus Epiphanies reigned over the Middle Eastern division which included the land of Israel and Syria. He set up a military garrison in Jerusalem to oversee the Hellenization of Israel and the Jewish people, forcing them to turn away from worshiping the God of Israel. The event of *Hanukkah* and the rededication of the Temple took place in 165 BC in Israel within this political setting.

Antiochus brought in many laws to enforce Greek worship over the land and he forbade any form of Biblical worship. On the 25th of *Kislev* 165 BC, he ordered statues of the Greek gods Zeus and Jupiter to be set up in the Temple in Jerusalem and a law was passed that all the people of Israel were to bow down and worship these statues. Any disobedience would be punished by death. Many Jewish people died, while a large number converted to Greek worship in order to save their lives.

During Antiochus' reign of terror he ordered the murder of the High Priest, Onais, many Jewish people fled from Jerusalem and other cities to hide in caves and hills, fearing for their lives. He made laws which interfered with every aspect of Jewish life. He forbade the practice of keeping *Shabbat* as a holy day for worshipping God and celebrating of the Biblical holidays. He banned the study of the Scriptures and prohibited the custom of circumcision as well. Instead he ordered the sacrifice of pigs on the altar of the Temple and the holy objects in the Temple were knocked over or stolen. The *Menorah*, the lampstand that was to shine in the Temple at all times, was knocked down. People were forced to change their names from Hebrew names to Greek versions such as Joshua was changed to Jason.

The Greek-Assyrian soldiers set about bribing Jewish children with money to disobey their parents, to bow down to Greek gods and to stop studying the Scriptures. Jewish parents in turn gave their children money to stay faithful to God and Jewish children themselves invented a game using a spinning top so they could keep learning the Scriptures. Boys were required to learn the first five books of the Bible by heart and would study in groups to learn these passages.

They continued to study in their groups but when they heard the footsteps of the soldiers approaching, they would quickly pull out their spinning top and pretend they were playing a game. They would spin the top for rewards. Once the soldiers had left, they would carry on learning the passages of the *Torah* together.

In a village called Modiin, not far from Jerusalem, an enforcement officer called Apelles gathered all the people together in the centre for a ceremony to sacrifice a pig on an altar and the villagers were to swear allegiance to Antiochus. A man called Mattiyahu, who was a respected member of the community and the head of a priestly Hashmonite family, refused to take part, preferring to remain loyal to God. He confronted Apelles the soldier when he refused to participate and in the confrontation killed the soldier. He had to flee to the hills around Jerusalem for his safety and his five sons and their families followed him. He sent back a message to the people of Modiin saying "whoever is for God follow me". This started the Maccabean uprising against the Greek-Assyrian soldiers and their leaders.

The name Maccabees is an acronym for Hebrew words in the Bible, *"Who among the gods is like you, O Lord?"* (*Exodus 15:11)* which became their banner in battle.

From the hills around Jerusalem and the valleys of Judea, the Maccabees fought the soldiers with Judah, one of Mattiyahu's son leading the battles. They only had stones and farm tools to fight with but took advantage of knowing the land better than the soldiers and fought until they defeated them.

The Greek soldiers were driven out of Jerusalem and the Temple on the 25th of *Kislev,* three years after the initial desecration of the Temple with the statues of the Greek gods. The Maccabees started to clear the Temple of the Greek gods. The *Menorah* which had been knocked down was put back in place. According to laws in Leviticus the *Menorah* should be lit continually before the Lord in the Temple (*Leviticus 24:1-4).* In order to do this, they needed to relight it. They searched amongst the ruins in the Temple for consecrated oil but found enough oil to light the Menorah for only one day.

The miracle that occurred was that once the *Menorah* was relit the oil lasted for eight days giving the Temple priests enough time to prepare more consecrated oil and so re-establish Temple worship. There was great rejoicing when a new altar was set up and the Temple was rededicated to God.

Lessons about God through the holiday of *Hanukkah*

Defend faith and worship of the living God

The people of Israel learnt the importance of defending their faith and beliefs, their worship and way of life. If they had not taken a stand against the Greek leaders, they would have been forced to follow false worship, and lose true worship of God. Instead, they overcame an enemy who sought to destroy their faith and the faith of their children. Jewish parents sought to keep their children loyal to true worship of God. Children themselves invented games so they could still keep studying the Word of God.

God provided a miracle

In the midst of their struggle to remain faithful to God, God intervened on behalf of his people and encouraged them by providing enough oil to last for eight days. True worship of God in the Temple was established again.

The way Jewish people celebrate *Hanukkah*

Jewish people have been celebrating the holiday since 165 BC after the rededication of the Temple to God. In the evening a candlestick called a *Hanukkiyah* is lit. The *Hanuykkiyah* is the same shape as the Menorah in the Temple, to symbolise the *Menorah*. It has eight candle holders, with an extra taller candle holder in the middle. The candle in the middle is used to light the other candles and is called the *Shamash* or servant candle.

On the first night one candle is lit, then another each night until all eight candles are lit by the last evening. Each evening after the candle lighting the *Hanukkiyah* is put on a window ledge so that the light will shine out into the darkness as a witness to God's miracle. Blessings are read as the candles are kindled, to thank God for the miracle at *Hanukkah*.

Songs are sung which tell of God's victory. Stories are told to remember the Maccabees' determination to defend their worship of God. Children play games with a spinning top called a *Sevivon*, just like the ones children used during the uprising against the Greek-Assyrian soldiers. On each side of the *Sevivon* there is a Hebrew letter which stands for a Hebrew word making the sentence, "A great miracle took place here".

During the holiday children are given money or gifts each day. Food made with oil, to remember the oil in the Temple, such as doughnuts or *latkis* which are grated potato cakes are eaten.

How the holiday relates to Jesus' teaching and ministry

We know from the book of John that Jesus was in Jerusalem around the Temple area during the holiday of Hanukkah,

> *Then came the Feast of Dedication at Jerusalem. It was winter and Jesus was in the Temple area walking in Solomon's Colonnade. (John 10:22-23)*

In that passage in John, people were asking Jesus if he was the Messiah and he answered by referring to the miracles he did in his Father's name,

> *The Jews gathered round him, saying, "How long will you keep us in suspense? If you are the Christ (Messiah), tell us plainly." Jesus answered, "I did tell you, but you do not believe. The miracles I do in my Father's name speak for me...My sheep listen to my voice, I know them and they follow me."*
> *(John 10:24-25,27)*

It was appropriate that Jesus was referring to the miracles he had done in God's name because *Hanukkah* was a time when people would have been thinking about the miracle that occurred during *Hanukkah.* Jesus had performed many miracles demonstrating who he was and God's love for people.

As Jesus walked around Solomon's colonnade in the Temple area he would have seen all the *Hanukkiyahs* on the window ledges. The *Hanukkiyahs* were made of clay pots and wicks in Jesus' day, with olive oil inside to light them. The homes in Jerusalem were built closely together and when the *Hanukkiyas* were lit, the lights would have shone out together, bringing a glowing light into the darkness of the night sky.

Light is an important part of *Hanukkah* and it is also called the Holiday of Lights. Jesus said,

> *"I am the light of the world. Whoever follows me will never walk in darkness, but will have the light of Light." (John 8:12)*

Jesus brought spiritual light to everyone who follows him so they would never walk in darkness again but have the light of God, fulfilling a prophecy from Isaiah,

> *The people walking in darkness have seen a great light; on those living in the land of darkness a light has dawned. (Isaiah 9:2)*

Jesus taught his followers that they too must be light to other people as a witness for God, shining for him and bringing his light to those living in darkness,

> *"You are the light of the world. A city on a hill cannot be hidden. Neither do people light a lamp and put it under a bowl. Instead they put it on its stand and it*

gives light to everyone in the house ... "
(Matthew 5:14-16)

Jesus also said for his followers to live as children of light,

For once you were children of darkness, but now you
are light in the Lord. Live as children of the light.
(Ephesians 5:8)

The spiritual lessons of the holiday and how they apply to us today

We can learn much from the holiday of *Hanukkah* and its values are still relevant for us today.

Defend our Faith and our beliefs

The people of Israel had to take a stand to defend their faith and worship of God as Antiochus forcibly took over the Temple and tried to destroy true worship and following the Bible.

We too need to defend our faith and Biblical values, there is so much in our society trying to replace our belief in God and compromise our walk with him. In our fellowships we must stand for the truth of God's Word and not let worldly or cultural values take over, praying for courage to take our stand.

Do not conform to the pattern of this world, but be
transformed by the renewing of your mind. Then you
will be able to test and approve what God's will is –
his good, pleasing and perfect will.
(Romans 12:2)

Protecting our children

Another message that comes through the story of *Hanukkah* is the importance of protecting children from forces that would lead them astray from God and his ways. The Greek-Assyrian soldiers tried to bribe the Jewish children with money to bow down and worship idols.

Guarding children in their faith and teaching them about the Bible is important so they can follow God. There is so much pressure and temptation to lead children away within school and education which undermines godly values. We need to teach them that it is better to follow the Lord and he will honour them as they honour him. We need to encourage children to stand for their belief in God.

God will provide the oil

God provided enough oil so the light of the *Menorah* could continue to shine, and worship could be renewed in the Temple. It is interesting that God provided the oil supernaturally. Oil is often used for anointing in the Bible, bringing the supernatural power of God into someone's life so they can serve him. God will provide for us supernaturally, so we can serve him. The Bible says,

> *You, O Lord, keep my lamp burning. (Psalm 18:28)*

Cleansing of the Temple – our bodies, the temple of the Holy Spirit

In several verses we are told that our bodies are the temple of God and that the Holy Spirit dwells within us.

> *Do you not know that your bodies are temples of the Holy Spirit, who is in you, whom you have received*

from God...Therefore honour God with your bodies.
(1 Corinthians 6:19-20)

Recognising that we are the temple of God where the Holy Spirit dwells, we should seek to remove idols in our lives just as the People of Israel had to take down idols from the Temple in Jerusalem. There may be idols that are preventing us from worshipping God and serving him with our whole heart. We can ask God to reveal what these idols are, and then pray to get rid of them from our lives.

Therefore my dear friends, flee from idolatry.
(1 Corinthians 10:14)

For God did not call us to be impure, but to live a holy life. (Thessalonians 4:7)

It is not only idols but also sin that hinders us. God warns us not to grieve the Holy Spirit and to rid ourselves of sin,

And do not grieve the Holy Spirit of God, with whom you were sealed for the day of redemption. Get rid of all bitterness, rage and anger, brawling and slander, along with every form of malice. Be kind and compassionate to one another, forgiving each other, just as in Christ God forgave you.
(Ephesians 4:30-32)

Galatians gives a list of sins that damages us and our relationship with God and could compromise the plans and purposes he has for our lives.

Sexual immorality, impurity and debauchery; idolatry and witchcraft; hatred, discord, jealousy, fits of rage, selfish ambition, dissensions, factions and envy; drunkenness, orgies, and the like.
(Galatians 5:19-20)

When sin has come into either our lives or our fellowships we need to repent so we can be restored to freedom in our walk with God,

> *Let us purify ourselves from everything that contaminates body and spirit. (2 Corinthians 7:12)*

Rededicating ourselves to him as an act of worship

Having repented from sin and praying for idols in our lives to be removed, we can rededicate our lives to God in a similar way as the Temple was rededicated in Jerusalem for true worship to continue.

> *Those who cleanse themselves from the latter will be instruments for special purposes, made holy, useful to the Master and prepared to do any good work. (Timothy 2:21)*

Pray that the fruits of the Spirit to be in us and we would be led by the Spirit.

> *...the fruit of the Spirit is love, joy, patience, kindness, goodness, faithfulness, gentleness and self-control. Against such things there is no law...since we live by the Spirit, let us keep in step with the Spirit. (Galatians 5:22,23,25)*

Jesus is "the light of the world", and we are to be light in darkness

Just as the *Hanukkah* candles would be lit and give light in the darkness, so followers of Jesus are called to be witnesses in the darkness by shining his light. Jesus, the light of the world, revealed God's love and we are reminded to let his light shine through us into the world around us.

For God, who said, "Let light shine out of darkness," made his light shine in our hearts to give us the light of the knowledge of God's glory displayed in the face of Christ. (2 Corinthians 4:6)

In the same way, let your light shine before others, that they may see your good deeds and glorify your Father in heaven. (Matthew 5:16)

Main Message

The holiday of *Hanukkah* is the story of rededication to God. It tells of God's supernatural provision of oil in the Temple, so true worship could be restored. The holiday draws attention to the importance of defending our faith, protecting the faith of our children as well as our places of worship from worldly and ungodly practices. Through the holiday we are encouraged to stand for righteousness knowing God will honour us just as he provided the oil for the *Menorah* so worship could continue. God will provide for us supernaturally by the anointing of the Holy Spirit.

We are encouraged to pray for our cleansing from sin and to rededicate our lives and bodies as the Temple of the Holy Spirit to be used by God. Also, to let the Holy Spirit lead our lives to become witnesses for him in the darkness of the world around us.

During the holiday the *Hanukkiyah* is placed on a window ledge against the window to let the light shine out bearing witness to the miracle God did in the Temple long ago. We can light the *Hanukkiyah* and place it on our window ledge or light a Christmas candle as Christmas is so close to *Hanukkah* and let the light remind us that Jesus is the light of the world and his light is a powerful light within us shining out as a witness to the world in darkness.

It was lovely for us to see the candles in the *Hanukkiyahs* shine out of homes into the dark skies at wintertime in Israel.

Prayer

Heavenly Father, please give me the grace and steadfastness to stand for you in all that I face in this world. Please fill me with your Holy Spirit to live for you and be a witness for you. Let your light shine bringing people out of darkness. Amen.

Prayer of salvation

You may have been touched by reading about God's salvation plan through the Holidays in *Yeshua,* Jesus. If you would like to come into a relationship with the Messiah, all you need to do is pray to know him. God showed his incredible love and he made a way for all people to come into a relationship with him.

Dear Heavenly Father,

I believe Yeshua, the Passover Lamb, died for my sins and his blood was shed to set me free. I believe he made atonement for me and that nothing can separate me from a relationship with you. I am sorry and I repent. Please forgive all my sins and bring me into a relationship with you. I pray to be filled with the Holy Spirit in the same way the disciples were filled at Shavuot, Pentecost. I pray to live a Spirit led life.

In Yeshua's name.

Amen

A Note From The Author

I wrote this book to bless Christians. It is my hope that you will enjoy reading about the Biblical Holidays and understand the Bible in a deeper way.

If you would like to celebrate them, I hope you take joy in doing so. If you would like to read about them only, be blessed in that too!

The Bible tells us,

> *Therefore, do not let anyone judge you by what you eat or drink, or with regard to a religious festival, a new moon celebration or a Sabbath day. (Colossians 2:16)*

My prayer is that you draw closer to God and gain more understanding of his incredible plan for us by reading this book.

Every blessing,

Melanie Moscovich

About The Book Cover

When I was thinking about the book cover and what it should look like I thought about all the blessings God gave to his people Israel and his followers in Christ. His love, freedom from slavery, the harvests and his provision, the Written Word, Jesus' sacrifice and the Holy Spirit. All so important and I was thinking about getting these into a picture.

I decided to pray specifically about the book cover and the city of Jerusalem came into my mind. I realised Jerusalem plays such an important role in the holidays. God required the people of Israel to celebrate and worship him in Jerusalem for three of the holidays and the book of Revelations tells us we will again worship him there in the future. Jesus' sacrifice as the Lamb of God took place nearby Jerusalem, and the Holy Spirit came to Jerusalem to his disciples waiting there.

I knew I should include Jerusalem on the cover. I liked the idea of many people being drawn to God from all over the world and being blessed through what God has demonstrated in the holidays. The picture on the cover is actually based on a picture we have in our home. It was the first picture Ofer and I bought when we were newly married and living in Israel. A Jewish man who had recently made *Aliyah* from Russia was selling his pictures from door to door to raise money to make a living in Israel. We were delighted to buy one of his pictures and it has been with us in our home ever since.

Acknowledgements

Thank you to everyone who has supported me and prayed for the writing of this book. I appreciate what you have given so much.

I would especially like to thank Mairi Lucas for your wonderful artwork which has brought something so special to the book. Your work has been such a blessing to me and I appreciate your friendship and prayers over the many years we have known each other.

I want to thank my Mum, Joy Wright, for your help, support and prayers. Also, thanks to Dorothe Kauffman for proof reading and your advice for this book.

Thank you as well to Judy Johnson for reading through and your prayers.

Special thanks to Rev Denise Binks and Dr Yohanan Stanfield, for your commendations. Thank you to Becky Bouker for endorsing my writing and for your friendship.

Thank you to Ambra Vivian for your commendation and bringing this to a much younger generation.

Thank you to Eleni Syndica-Drummond for the portrait photo. Thank you as well to Phoebe Booth, for your help. A big thank you to Jan Holdaway for your skill and help in getting this book published.

I would especially like to thank my husband Ofer and our three children, Koren, Adi and Gideon for all your encouragement and many prayers which overcame all challenges.

Adi, all the help you gave is so appreciated.

Thank you, Lord, for your incredible love and sacrifice demonstrated through the Biblical Holidays may we cherish the holidays always.

Melanie

Also by Melanie Moscovich

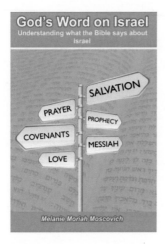

God's Word on Israel, Melanie Moscovich's first book gives the reader a clear understanding of what God says about Israel in the Bible covering topics that all Christians need to know about regarding Israel.

Each chapter has a look at a relevant Biblical subject related to Israel such as: God's plan for the Jewish people; how God has used Israel; the relationship between the body of Christ and Israel and also what God is doing in Israel today.

The reader is given insight into God's Word and will for Israel and how to pray for Israel in line with the scriptures. God's faithfulness to his Word and promises are clearly demonstrated throughout book and will greatly encourage Christians who put their trust in the Bible.

Contact Melanie at: mm.moscovich@gmail.com
http://:mmmoscovich.wix.com/book